PEARSON ALWAYS LEARNING

2

STUDENT BOOK

Tropical Island

Laura Miller • José Luis Morales
Series Advisor: David Nunan

Series Consultants:
Hilda Martínez • Xóchitl Arvizu

Advisory Board:
Tim Budden • Tina Chen • Betty Deng • Aaron Jolly • Dr. Nam-Joon Kang
Dr. Wonkey Lee • Wenxin Liang • Ann Mayeda • Wade O. Nichols • Jamie Zhang

Pearson Education Limited
Edinburgh Gate
Harlow
Essex CM20 2JE
England
and Associated Companies throughout the world.

Our Discovery Island ™

www.ourdiscoveryisland.com

Based on the work of Linnette Ansel Erocak

The rights of Laura Miller, José Luis Morales, and Linnette Ansel Erocak to be identified as authors of this work have been asserted by them in accordance with the Copyright, Designs and Patents Act 1988.

Stories on pages 16, 26, 38, 48, 60, 70, 82, and 92 by Steve Elsworth and Jim Rose. The rights of Steve Elsworth and Jim Rose to be identified as authors of this work have been asserted by them in accordance with the Copyright, Designs and Patents Act 1988.

Phonics syllabus and activities by Rachel Wilson

First published 2012
Seventeenth impression 2020

ISBN: 978-1-4479-0062-7

Set in Longman English 16/21pt

Printed in Malaysia (CTP-VVP)

Illustrators: Adam Clay, Leo Cultura, Joelle Dreidemy (The Bright Agency), Sue King (Plum Pudding), Stephenine Lau, Yam Wai Lun, Katie McDee, Bill McGuire (Shannon Associates), Jackie Stafford, Olimpia Wong, and Teddy Wong

Picture Credits: The Publishers would like to thank the following for their kind permission to reproduce their photographs: (Key: b-bottom; c-center, l-left; r-right; t-top) Alamy Images: 62 (5), Blend Images 28t (parents), 28tl, Corbis Super RF 94 (4), Design Pics Inc 94 (1), Tim Gainey 94 (3), Image Source 50br, 84cr, MIXA 40 (c); Trevor Clifford: 15l, 25l, 40 (a), 50t, 104, 105, 106; Corbis: Comstock 84cl, Joe McDonald 62 (4); Imagemore Co., Ltd: 15r; iStockphoto: alxpin 62 (sun), Eric Isselee 61t (4), 61t (5), Ju-Lee 61t (2), Zoran Kolundzija 18 (boat), Derek Latta 40 (f), Carolina K. Smith, M.D 62 (moon); Photolibrary.com: Comstock 94 (5), Glow Images, Inc 28cl, EA. Janes 62 (6), Mike Kenip 40 (h), Monkey Business Images Ltd 28c (parents), Photodisc 40 (e), Photos India 40 (d), George Shelley 28tr, Siepmann 50bc; Shutterstock. com: AGfoto 93 (bottle), aleks.k 62 (1), Bragin Alexey 69 (toast), Aaron Amat 71 (burgers), Andresr 47r, Andy Dean Photography 87tr, 87cr, Yuri Arcurs 28b (grandparents), 47l, 49l, 49r, 93r, Argunova 69 (corn), Silvano Audisio 18 (car), AVAVA 28bl, Alina Bakker 93 (books), Beata Becla 90 (e), Bernad 40 (i), Best Photo 1 94 (2), Andre Blais 72r, blessings 28b (baby), Boris15 68 (b), Uwe Bumann 84l, Alexey Chernitevich 68 (j), Dmitry Chernobrov 80 (i), Clemmesen 69 (raisins), Coprid 80 (e), Alexander Dashewsky 93 (CDs), Dimos 90 (b), Le Do 68 (h), 69 (pumpkin), dusan964 58 (b), Elenamiv 90 (a), Elena Elisseeva 93 (fruit), Elnur 80 (h), Christopher Elwell 71 (salad), Gelpi 40 (b), Mandy Godbehear 36 (g), Gorilla 36 (f), grafica 59r, grafikfoto 62 (2), Grauvision 71 (grapes), Hallgerd 40 (j), Johann Helgason 69 (cereal), Patrick Hermans 61b (4), Sony Ho 71 (beans), Iculig 80 (f), Imageman 68 (i), iofoto 25r, 87cl, IRA 71 (fish), Rafa Irusta 71 (chocolate), Eric Isselee 58 (c), 58 (d), 58 (e), 61t (3), 61bl, 61br, Jambostock 36 (h), Joingate 71 (milk), Michael Jung 59l, Olga Kadroff 80 (a), Karkas 61b (2), Kayros Studio 71 (pizza), Kesu 68 (d), Kirsanov 58 (a), Katja Kodba 61t (1), Lepas 71 (yoghurt), 80 (b), Jim Lopes 90 (c), Svetlana Lukienko 68 (f), Johnny Lye 71 (corn), Rob Marmion 72l, Stephen Mcsweeny 71 (hot dog), Cindy Minear 40 (g), Monkey Business Images 107l, 107r, Juriah Mosin 36 (b), Antonio Jorge Nunes 28t (twins), 28br, Nayashkova Olga 68 (e), ostill 40 (l), 47cr, Palmer Kane LLC 47t, Paul Matthew Photography 87tl, Denis Pepin 69 (nuts), Keith Publicover 72c, Jack Qi 28cr, Ruzanna 90 (d), Dario Sabljak 80 (g), Olga Sapegina 61b (1), Brad Sauter 47cl, Schankz 71 (banana), Elena Schweitzer 93 (toys), Sally Scott 69 (beans), SergiyN 91l, Dmitriy Shironosov 28c (twins), 36 (a), 61bc (chicken), Shkurd 93 (toothbrush), Alex Staroseltsev 68 (a), Magdalena Szachowska 36 (d), tatniz 68 (c), Robert Taylor 62 (3), Leah-Anne Thompson 40 (k), Suzanne Tucker 36 (c), 36 (e), Ultimathule 90 (f), Verdateo 80 (d), Darryl Vest 50bl, Popov Maxim Viktorovich 90 (g), Valentyn Volkov 71 (soda), Vaclav Volrab 71 (apple), Brian Weed 61b (3), Chamille White 80 (c), Willmetts 61bc (sheep), Lisa F. Young 84r, Julia Zakharova 68 (g); Thinkstock: Hemera Technologies 18 (ball).

Contents

Scope and sequence

Welcome

Vocabulary	**Time:** one o'clock, two o'clock, three o'clock, four o'clock, five o'clock, six o'clock, seven o'clock, eight o'clock, nine o'clock, ten o'clock, eleven o'clock, twelve o'clock **Daily routines:** wake up, get up, eat breakfast, go to school, eat lunch, eat dinner, go to bed
Structures	What time is it? It's one o'clock. I wake up at six o'clock.

1 My toys

Vocabulary	**Toys:** bike, car, train, boat, ball, doll, teddy bear, kite **Numbers:** sixteen, seventeen, eighteen, nineteen, twenty	**Values:** Friendship is important. **Cross-curricular:** **Math:** Plus, minus, and equals **Phonics: ch, sh** chop, chin, rich, much, ship, shell, fish, dish
Structures	What's this/that? It's a bike. It's yellow. What are these/those? They're bikes. They're yellow. How many bikes are there? There are sixteen bikes.	

2 My family

Vocabulary	**Family members:** uncle, aunt, son, daughter, grandson, granddaughter, cousin **Neighborhood places:** house, garden, store, bakery, post office, restaurant, bank, apartment	**Values:** Spend time with your relatives. **Cross-curricular:** **Social science:** Types of family members **Phonics: th,** th this, that, then, with, thin, thick, math, path
Structures	Who's he/she? He's/She's my uncle/aunt. Where's my/your uncle? Your/My uncle is in the house.	

3 Move your body

Vocabulary	**Actions:** touch, wave, clap, point, shake, stamp, move, nod **Physical abilities:** jump, swim, dance, climb, swing, stand on your head, do cartwheels, do the splits	**Values:** Exercise regularly. **Cross-curricular:** **Health:** Exercise actions **Phonics: ng, nk** sing, ring, ping, long, ink, sink, pink, thank
Structures	Touch your toes. Can you jump? Yes, I can. / No, I can't. Can he/she jump? Yes, he/she can. / No, he/she can't.	

4 My face

Vocabulary	**Parts of the body:** face, eyes, ears, nose, mouth, hair **Hairstyles:** long, short, curly, straight, dark, blond, neat, messy	**Values:** Respect differences. **Cross-curricular:** **Math:** Shapes **Phonics: ai, ee** tail, rain, mail, wait, see, feet, week, sheep
Structures	I have a small nose. He/She has a small nose. Do you have a small nose? Yes, I do. / No, I don't. Does he/she have a small nose? Yes, he/she does. / No, he/she doesn't. He/She has long hair. His/Her hair is long.	

5 Animals

Vocabulary	**Farm animals:** cow, goat, chicken, turkey, duck, sheep, horse **Wild animals:** bat, crow, skunk, owl, fox	**Values:** Respect animals. **Cross-curricular:** **Science:** Daytime and nighttime animals **Phonics:** **igh, oa** high, sigh, light, right, boat, coat, soap, goat
Structures	What's this/that? It has big eyes. It's black and white. It's a cow. Is it small? Yes, it is. / No, it isn't. Is it a bat? Yes, it is. / No, it isn't. Are the bats big? Yes, they are. / No, they aren't.	

6 Food

Vocabulary	**Food items:** pizza, chicken, fish, rice, eggs, burgers, hot dogs, apples, bananas, pineapple, coconut, pumpkin, corn, toast, cereal, grapes, beans, raisins, nuts	**Values:** Eat good food. Choose good snacks. **Cross-curricular:** **Social science:** Different cultures, different foods **Phonics:** **oo**, oo zoo, too, food, moon, book, foot, look, cook
Structures	What's your favorite food? My favorite food is pizza. I like chicken. I don't like fish. He/She likes pineapple for breakfast. He/She doesn't like pineapple for breakfast. Does he/she like pineapple for breakfast? Yes, he/she does. / No, he/she doesn't.	

7 Clothes

Vocabulary	**Clothes:** a skirt, a T-shirt, a dress, pants, socks, shoes, a shirt, a coat, a sweater, a hat, a cap, boots, pajamas, jeans, sneakers	**Values:** Be polite. **Cross-curricular:** **Social science:** Occupations and uniforms **Phonics:** **ar, ir, or, ur** car, shark, sir, girl, for, corn, fur, surf
Structures	I'm wearing a white skirt. I'm not wearing white pants. What do you want? I want a shirt, please. Do you want a blue shirt? Yes, I do. / No, I don't.	

8 Weather

Vocabulary	**Weather:** cloudy, snowy, rainy, windy, sunny, cool **Days of the week:** Sunday, Monday, Tuesday, Wednesday, Thursday, Friday, Saturday	**Values:** Share with friends and family. **Cross-curricular:** **Science:** Temperature **Phonics:** **ow, oy** owl, now, cow, down, boy, toy, joy, cowboy
Structures	Do you like sunny days? Yes, I do. / No, I don't. I like cloudy days. I don't like cloudy days. What day is today? It's Sunday. What's the weather like? It's sunny.	

Welcome

1 Listen and write. A:02

2 Listen and point. A:03

3 Look and match.

1 yellow

2 green

3 orange

4 red

5 blue

6 pink

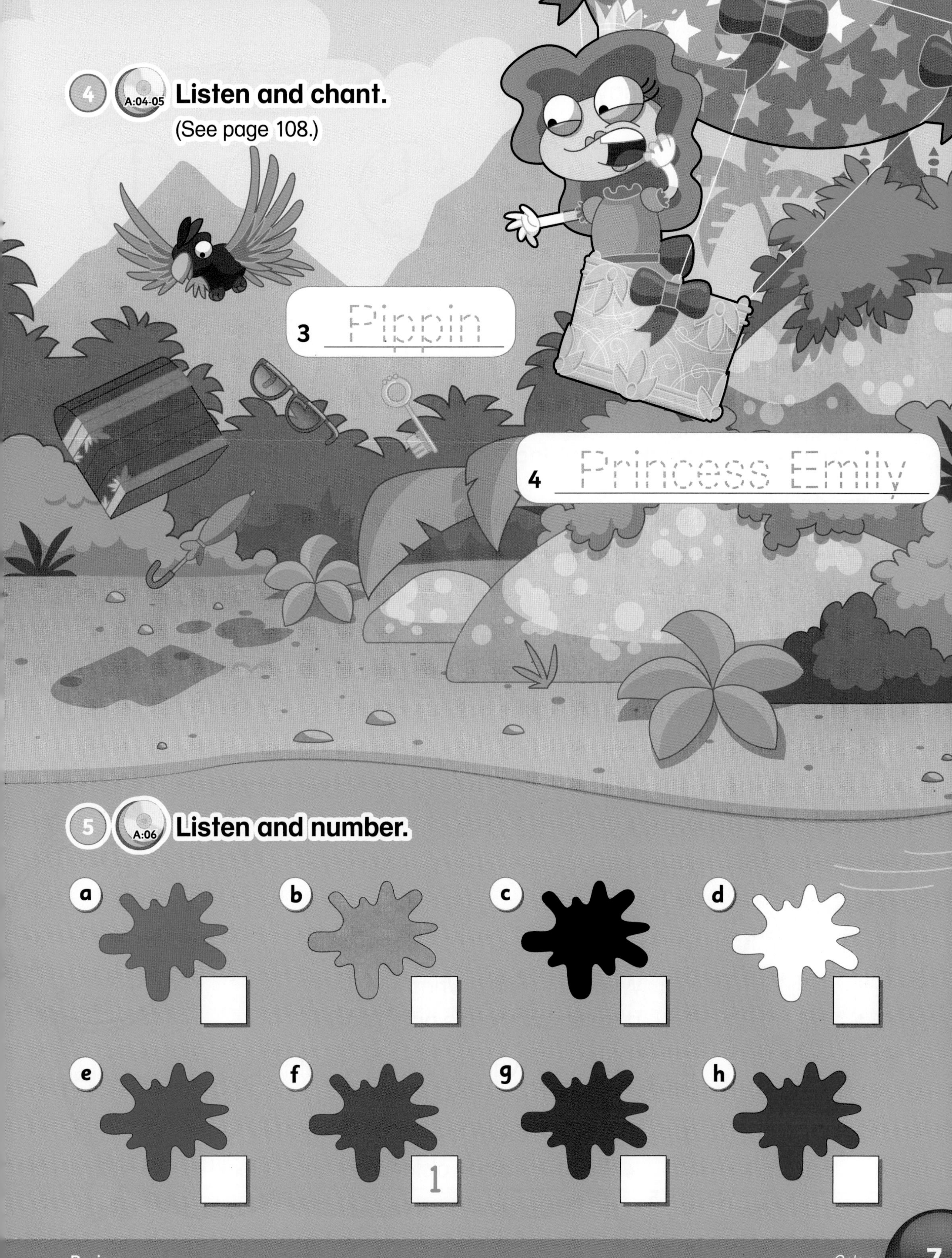

4 A:04-05 Listen and chant.
(See page 108.)
3 Pippin
4 Princess Emily
5 A:06 Listen and number.
a
b
c
d
e
f 1
g
h

6 A:07 Listen and say.

one o'clock	**two o'clock**	**three o'clock**	**four o'clock**	**five o'clock**	**six o'clock**

seven o'clock	**eight o'clock**	**nine o'clock**	**ten o'clock**	**eleven o'clock**	**twelve o'clock**

7 A:08-09 Listen and chant. Then draw.

CHANT

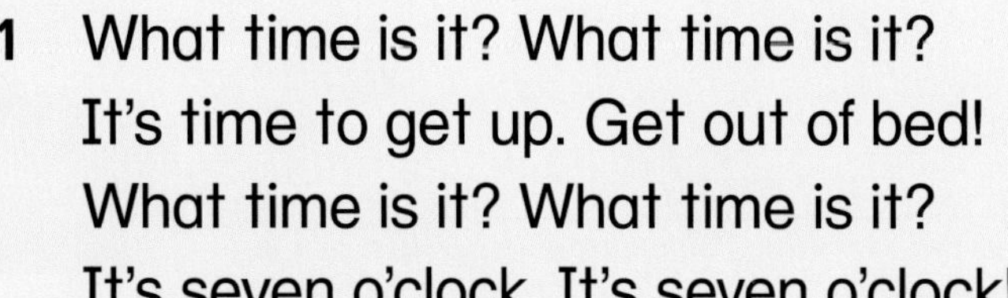

1 What time is it? What time is it?
It's time to get up. Get out of bed!
What time is it? What time is it?
It's seven o'clock. It's seven o'clock!

2 What time is it? What time is it?
It's time to go to school, my friend!
What time is it? What time is it?
It's eight o'clock. It's eight o'clock!

3 What time is it? What time is it?
It's time to eat lunch. I want some bread!
What time is it? What time is it?
It's one o'clock. It's one o'clock!

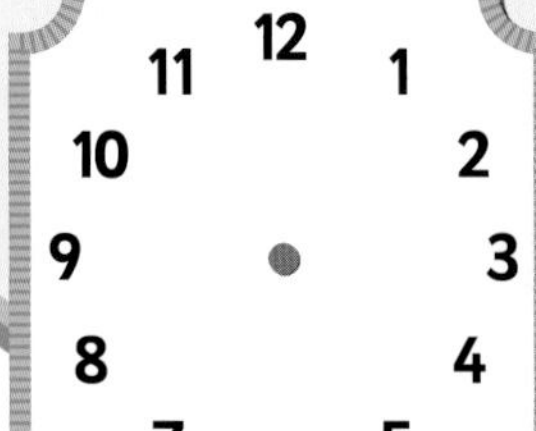

4 What time is it? What time is it?
It's time to go to bed, sleepy head!
What time is it? What time is it?
It's ten o'clock. It's ten o'clock!

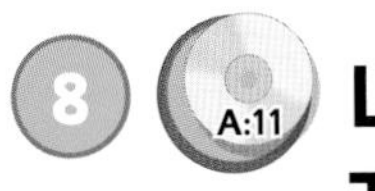

8 Listen and circle. Then ask and answer.

What time is it?	It's one o'clock.

1

2

3

4

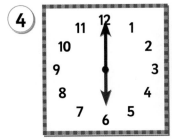

What time is it?

It's four o'clock.

9 Look and write.

1

It's ____________ o'clock.

2

It's ____________ o'clock.

3

It's ____________ o'clock.

10 A:12 Look, listen, and number.

VOCABULARY

a
wake up

b
get up

c
eat breakfast

d
go to school

e
eat lunch

f
eat dinner

g
go to bed

11 A:13 Listen and match. Then write.

1	wake up	twelve o'clock	I ______ at twelve o'clock.
2	get up	seven o'clock	I ______ at seven o'clock.
3	eat breakfast	five o'clock	I ______ at five o'clock.
4	go to school	eight o'clock	I ______ at eight o'clock.
5	eat lunch	six o'clock	I wake up at six o'clock.
6	eat dinner	nine o'clock	I ______ at nine o'clock.
7	go to bed	ten o'clock	I ______ at ten o'clock.

12 Look and write about yourself.

A:14 LOOK!
I wake up at six o'clock.

1 I wake up at ________ o'clock.

2 I get up at ________________.

3 I eat ________ at ________ o'clock.

4 I go to ________ at ________.

5 I ________ at ________.

13 A:15 Listen and sing. Circle. Then stick on page 7.

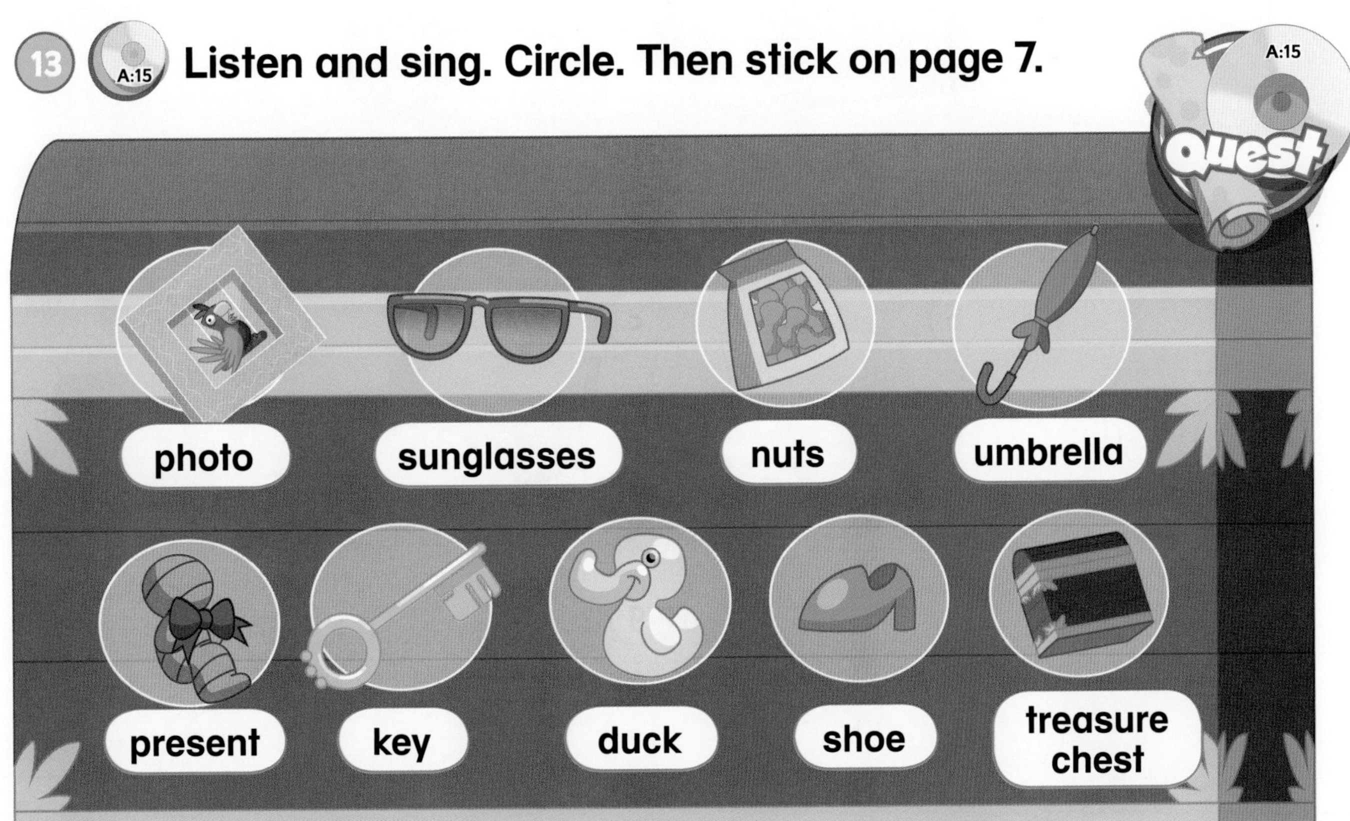

1 My toys

1 A:16 Listen.

2 A:17 Listen and say.

3 A:18 Listen and number.

a bike

b car

c train

d boat

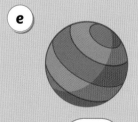

e ball

f doll

g teddy bear

h kite

4 A:19-20 **Listen and chant.** (See page 108.)

1

A:21 **LOOK!**

What's this/that?	It's a bike. It's yellow.
What are these/those?	They're bikes. They're yellow.

5 A:22 **Listen and number. Then ask and answer.**

A:23 Quest

6 A:24 **Listen and say.**

16	17	18	19	20
sixteen	seventeen	eighteen	nineteen	twenty

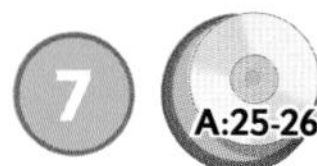

7 A:25-26 **Listen and write. Then sing.**

SONG

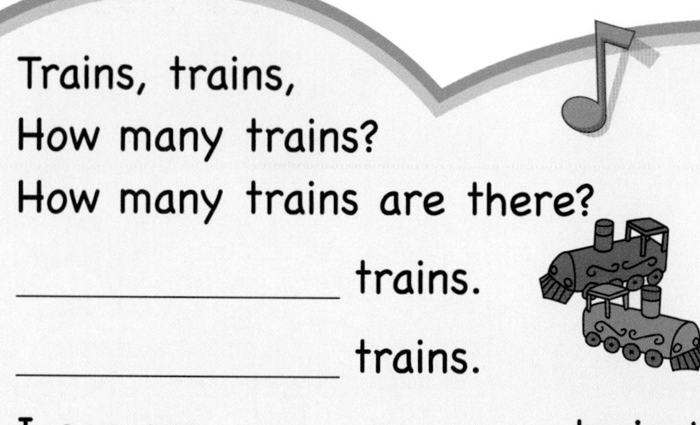

Trains, trains,
How many trains?
How many trains are there?
____________ trains.
____________ trains.
I can see ____________ trains!

Cars, cars,
How many cars?
How many cars are there?
____________ cars.
____________ cars.
I can see ____________ cars!

Balls, balls,
How many balls?
How many balls are there?
____________ balls.
____________ balls.
I can see ____________ balls!

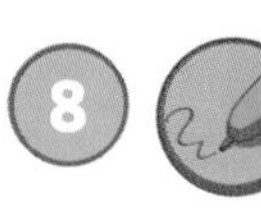
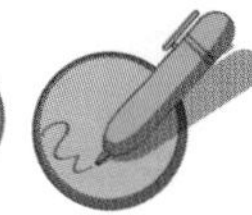

8 Look and circle. Then ask and answer.

How many bikes are there?

There are sixteen bikes.

1

nineteen / fifteen

2

seventeen / sixteen

3

twelve / twenty

4
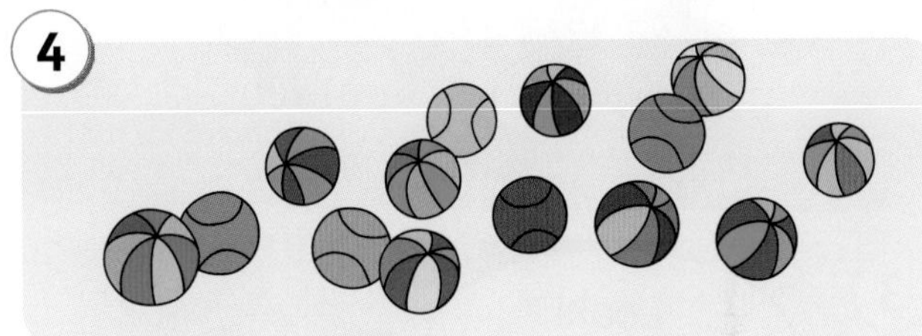

fourteen / eighteen

How many trains are there?

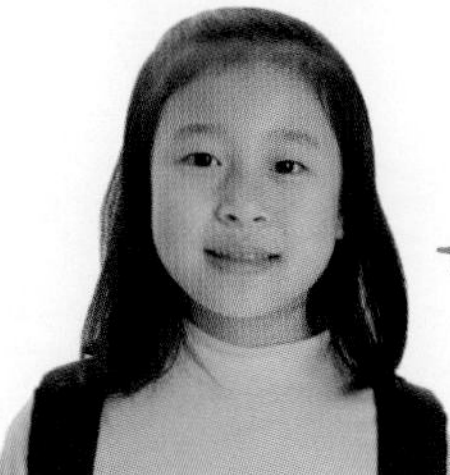

There are nineteen trains.

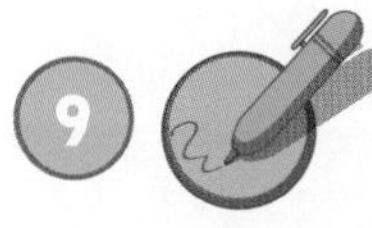

9 Look at Activity 8. Write.

1 How many trains are there?
There are ______________ trains.

2 How many teddy bears are there?
There ______________________________.

3 How many dolls are there?
There ______________________________.

4 How many balls are there?
There ______________________________.

Listen to the story.

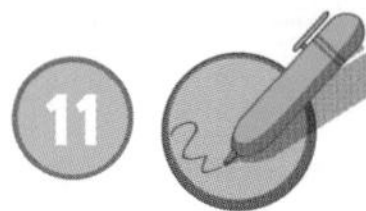

11 Look and circle.

1 (He's / She's) my friend.

2 (Lindy / Joe) is my friend.

3 (Lindy / Pippin) is my friend.

4 (Joe / Lindy) is my friend.

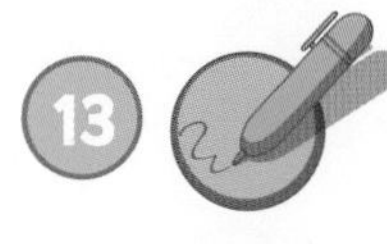

12 Role-play the story.

VALUES
Friendship is important.

13 Look and check (✓). Then write about yourself.

1

Good friends play together and share toys.

2

Good friends listen and help.

Who is your best friend? What do you like?

_____________ is my best friend.

We like ______________________

but we don't like _____________.

PARENT

HOME-SCHOOL LINK

Tell your family about your friends.

14 Look and write.

1	2	3	4	5	6	7	8		10
11		13		15		17	18		20

15 A:29 Listen and stick. Then say.

Stick

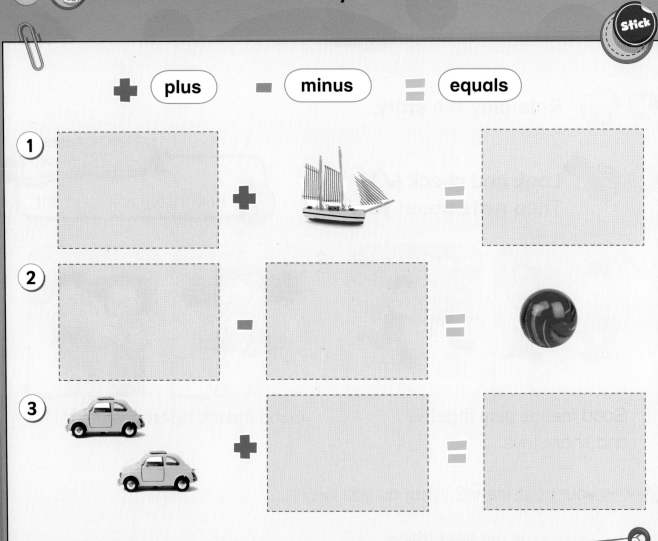

+ plus − minus = equals

1 + =

2 − =

3 + =

MINI-PROJECT
Draw a math problem for a friend.

  **Listen.**

1  **ch**

2  **sh**

  **Listen, point, and say.**

 **Listen and blend the sounds.**

1	ch - o - p	chop			2	ch - i - n	chin		
3	r - i - ch	rich			4	m - u - ch	much		
5	sh - i - p	ship			6	sh - e - ll	shell		
7	f - i - sh	fish			8	d - i - sh	dish		

19 **Underline *ch* and *sh*. Read the words aloud.**

1 shell

2 chop

3 rich

4 fish

5 chin

6 ship

20 A:33 **Listen. Then play and color.**

HAVE FUN!

Finish

15

14

13
16, 17,
x, x, x

12

9

10

11
It's a train.
It's brown.

8

7

6
They're bikes.
They're yellow.

5

Start

1

2

3
It's a ball.
It's blue.

4
14, 15, x,
x, 18

21 A:34 **Listen and point.**

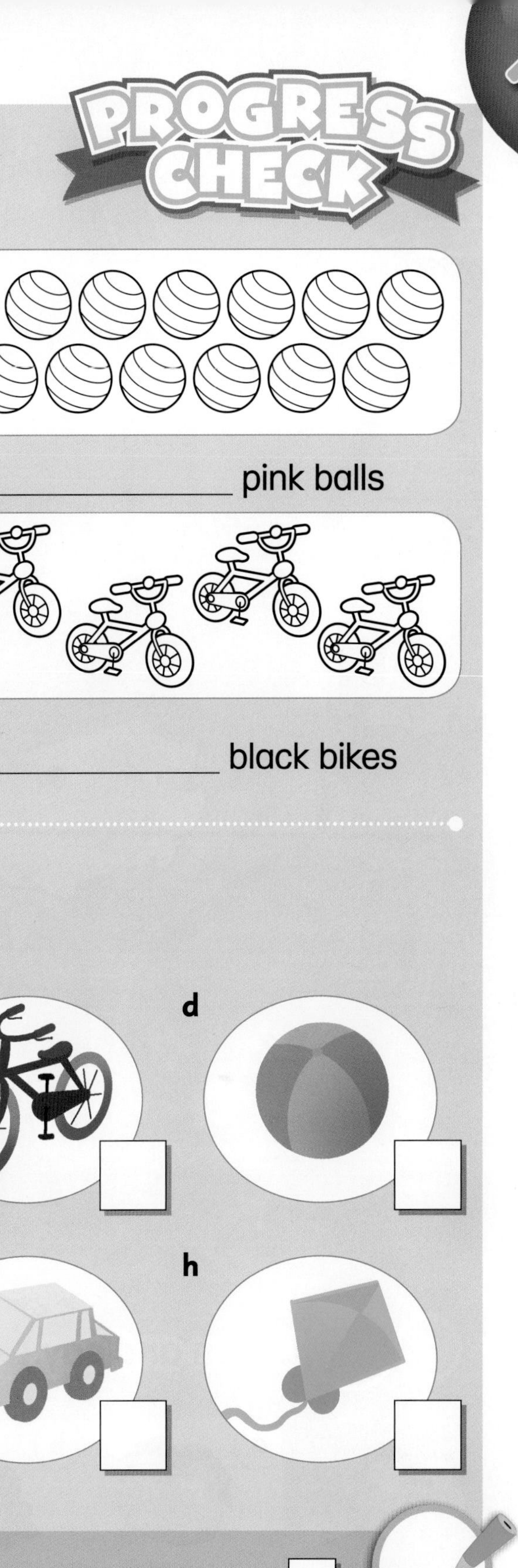

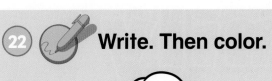

22 **Write. Then color.**

1  one brown doll

2 ________ pink balls

3 ________ red trains

4 ________ black bikes

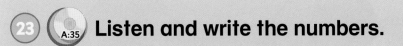

23 A:35 **Listen and write the numbers.**

a

b 14

c

d

e

f

g

h

I CAN

I can talk about toys.

I can count to twenty.

TEACHER

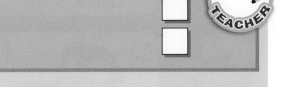

Now go to Tropical Island.

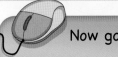

2 My family

1 A:36 Listen.

2 A:37 Listen and say.

3 A:38 Listen and number.

4 A:39-40 Listen and chant. (See page 108.)
A:41 LOOK!
Who's he/she?
He's/She's my uncle/aunt.
Who's = Who is
5 A:42 Listen and number. Then say.
a
b
c
A:43
Quest
He's my grandson.

6 A:44 **Stick. Then listen and say.**

a house
b garden
c store
d bakery
e post office
f restaurant
g bank
h apartment

7 A:45-46 **Listen and write. Then sing.**

Where's my grandma? Where's my grandma?
She's in the ____________. Snore, snore, snore.
Where's my grandma? Where's my grandma?
She's in the ____________. Snore, grandma, snore!

Where's my cousin? Where's my cousin?
He's in the ____________. Buy, buy, buy.
Where's my cousin? Where's my cousin?
He's in the ____________. Buy, cousin, buy!

Where's my daughter? Where's my daughter?
She's in the ____________. Count, count, count.
Where's my daughter? Where's my daughter?
She's in the ____________. Count, daughter, count!

Where's my uncle? Where's my uncle?
He's in the ____________. Eat, eat, eat.
Where's my uncle? Where's my uncle?
He's in the ____________. Eat, uncle, eat!

8 

Listen and match. Then ask and answer.

LOOK! A:47

Where's my uncle?	Your uncle is in the house.
Where's your uncle?	My uncle is in the house.

1 Where's my mom?

2 Where's my grandma?

3 Where's my uncle?

4 Where's my aunt?

5 Where's my grandson?

6 Where's my cousin?

BANK

BAKERY

Where's my mom?

Your mom is in the store.

9 

Complete for yourself. Then ask a friend.

SKILLS

grandma uncle aunt cousin

	POST OFFICE	BANK	BAKERY	STORE
Me				
My friend				

Where's your grandma?

My grandma is in the post office.

Listen to the story.

1
Ah! I love Princess Emily.

2
My mom and dad! Huh!
Hello, Emily.

3
My horrible brother ...
... and my horrible sister.

4
Grandpa and Grandma!

5
Family! Huh! And how many friends? One!

6
Pippin! Where are you?!

11 Look and write.

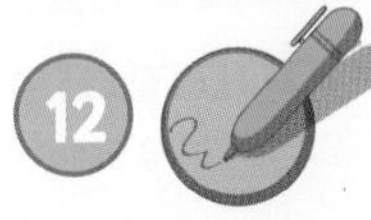

12 Read and circle.

1 Is Emily happy? Yes, she is. / No, she isn't.

2 Where are her mom and dad? They're in the (palace / bakery).

3 Where are her grandparents? They're in the (post office / garden).

13 Role-play the story.

VALUES

Spend time with your relatives.

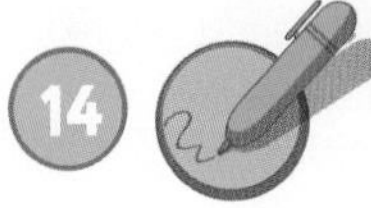

14 Read and write. Then draw your relatives.

How many aunts do you have?

____

How many uncles do you have?

____

How many cousins do you have?

____

HOME-SCHOOL LINK

Call or write to a relative who lives far away.

15 A:50 **Listen and point. Then say.**

young

baby

twins

parents

old

grandparents

16 **Look and match.**

twins parents babies grandparents

MINI-PROJECT

Make a poster about your family.

17 Listening A:51 Listen.

1  th

2  th

18 A:52 Listen, point, and say.

19 A:53 Listen and blend the sounds.

1 th - i - s this

2  th - a -  t that

3 th - e - n then

4 w - i - th with

5 th - i - n thin

6 th - i - ck thick

7 m - a - th math

8 p - a - th path

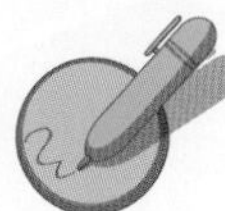

20 Underline *th*. Read the words aloud.

1 math

2 this

3 that

4 path

5 thick

6 thin

HAVE FUN!

21 A:54 **Listen. Then play.**

22 A:55 **Listen and act.**

Listen and check (✓).

1

a 

b 

2

a 

b 

3

a 

b 

4

a 

b 

5

a 

b 

6

a 

b 

7

a 

b 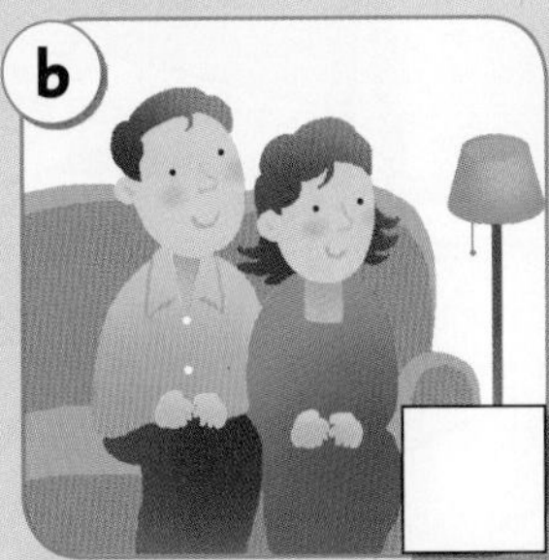

8

a 

b 

I can talk about my family. ☐

I can say where people are. ☐

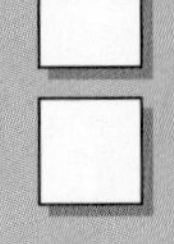

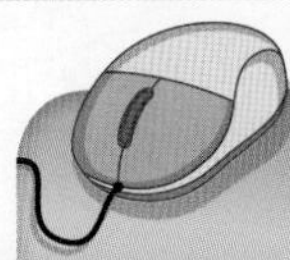

Now go to Tropical Island.

Review Units 1 and 2

1 A:57 **Listen. Then play.**

What's this/that?
What are these/those?
Where's my/
your ...?
What time
is it?
Who's he/she?
I ... at ...
o'clock.
How many ...
are there?
3
4
5
8
7
9
6
15
16
18
17
24
25
26
Finish

3 Move your body

1 A:58 Listen.

2 A:59 Listen and say.

3 A:60 Listen and number.

4 A:61-62 **Listen and chant.** (See page 108.)

A:63 **LOOK!**

Touch your toes.

5 A:64 **Listen and number. Then say.**

a

b

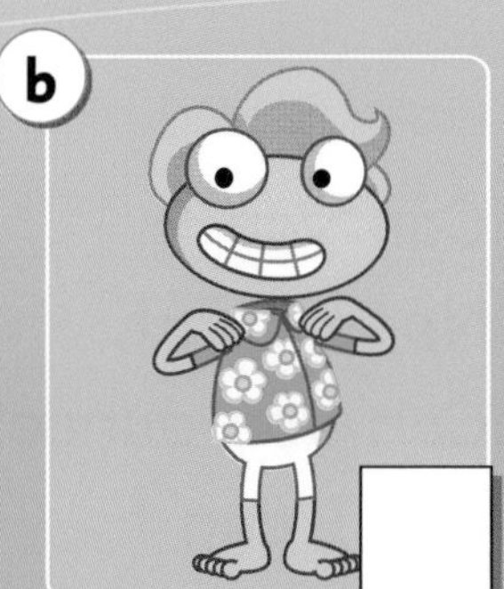

c

d

Shake your body.

6 Listen and say.

VOCABULARY

a 
jump

b 
swim

c 
dance

d 
climb

e 
swing

f 
stand on your head

g 
do cartwheels

h 
do the splits

7 Listen and write. Then sing.

SONG

Can you _________?
Yes, I can.
Can you jump?
Yes, I can.
Can you jump?
Yes, I can.
I can jump! Hooray!

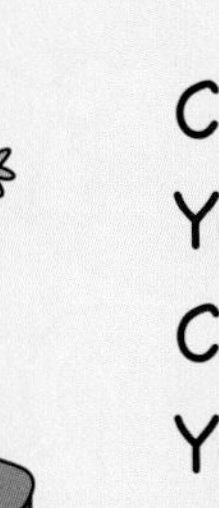
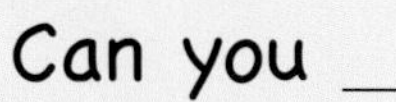

Can you _________?
Yes, I can.
Can you swim?
Yes, I can.
Can you swim?
Yes, I can.
I can swim! Hooray!

Can you _________?
No, I can't.
Can you climb?
No, I can't.
Can you climb?
No, I can't.
I can't climb. Boo hoo!

Can you _________?
No, I can't.
Can you dance?
No, I can't.
Can you dance?
No, I can't.
I can't dance. Boo hoo!

Can you jump?	Yes, I can. / No, I can't.
Can he/she jump?	Yes, he/she can. / No, he/she can't.

8 Look, read, and circle. Then ask and answer.

1 Can you do cartwheels?

Yes, I can.

No, I can't.

2 Can you do the splits?

Yes, I can.

No, I can't.

3 Can you swim?

Yes, I can.

No, I can't.

Can he do cartwheels?

Yes, he can.

9 Complete for yourself. Then ask a friend. SKILLS

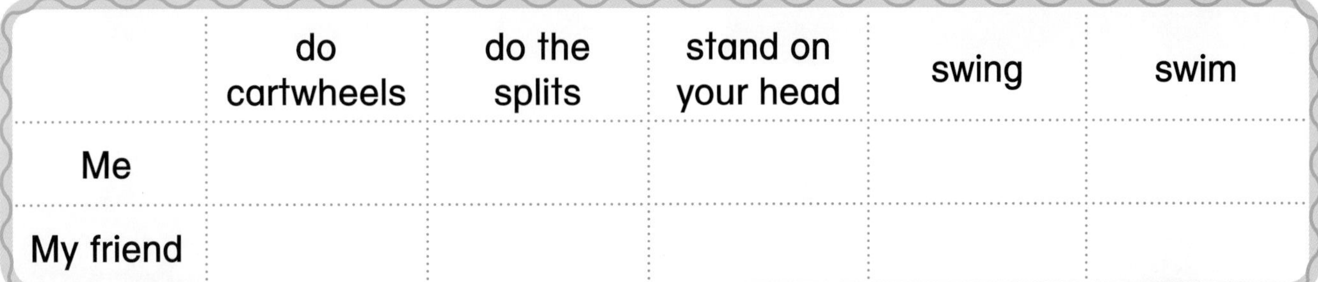

	do cartwheels	do the splits	stand on your head	swing	swim
Me					
My friend					

10 Write about yourself and ask a friend.

I can ____________________. I can't ____________________.

My friend can ____________________.

He / She can't ____________________.

A:70

Listen to the story.

12 Read and number. Then circle the speaker.

a Jump! Shake your body! ☐

b Jump! Jump! ☐

c Exercise is good for you. ☐

d Clap your hands! Stamp your feet! Touch your toes! ☐

or

13 Role-play the story.

14 Look and stick.

EXERCISE

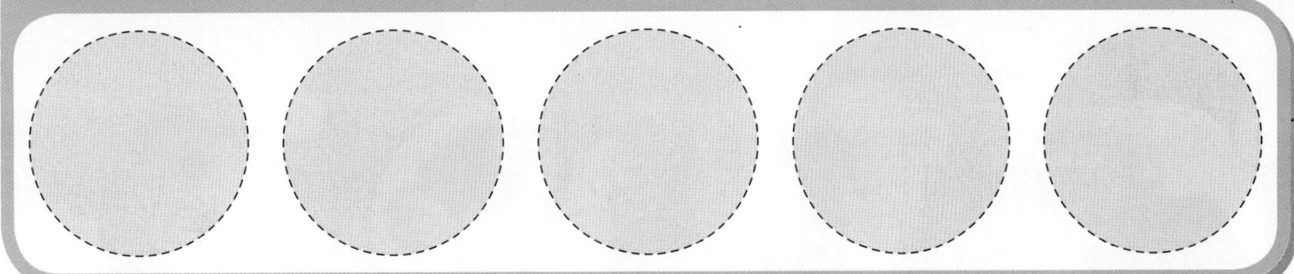

NOT EXERCISE

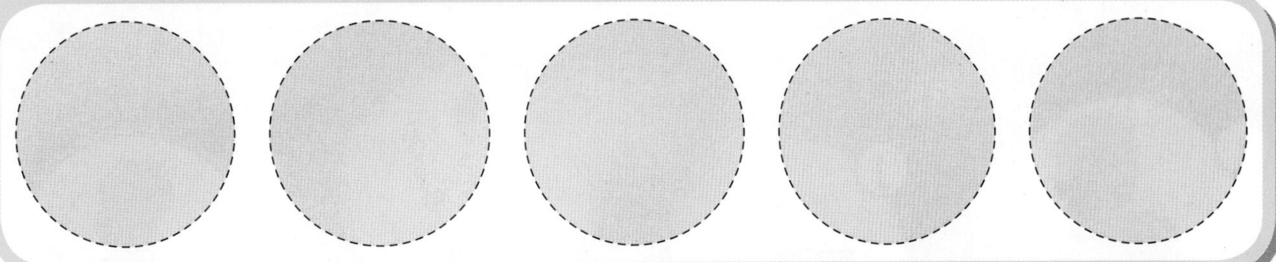

Draw a picture of yourself doing exercise. Show it to your family.

15 

Listen and number. Then say.

a 

pull

b

push

c 

hop

d 

skip

MINI-PROJECT

Work in small groups. Show the class an exercise.

16 

Listen and number. Then move.

a 

Clap your hands.

b 

Jump.

c 

Stamp your feet.

d 

Wave your arms.

e 

Move your head.

f 

Dance.

g 

Touch your toes.

h 

Shake your body.

i 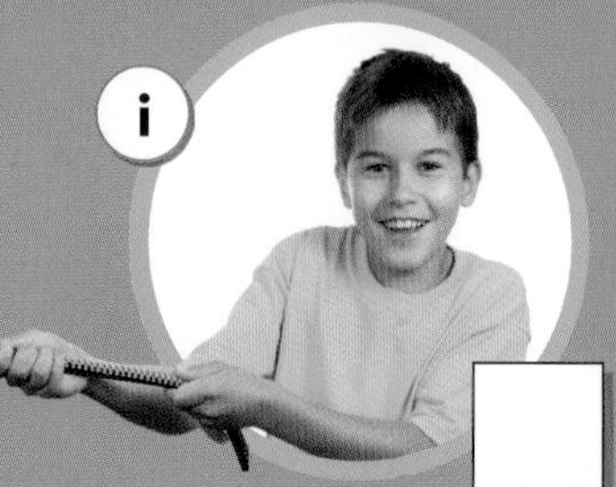

Pull.

j 

Push.

k 

Hop.

l 

Skip.

  17 A:73 **Listen.**

1 **ng** 2 **nk**

  18 A:74 **Listen, point, and say.**

 19 A:75 **Listen and blend the sounds.**

1	s - i - ng	sing		2	r - i - ng	ring
3	p - i - ng	ping		4	l - o - ng	long
5	i - nk	ink		6	s - i - nk	sink
7	p - i - nk	pink		8	th - a - nk	thank

 20 **Underline *ng* and *nk*. Read the words aloud.**

1 pink

2 sing

3 long

4 sink

5 ring

6 ink

21 A:76 **Listen. Then play.**

HAVE FUN!

Start

1 hands

2 arms

3 body

4 ? ☒

5 ? ☒

6 arms

7 head

8 toes

9 ? ☑

10 fingers

11 ☑

12 feet

13 legs

Finish

Listen and move.

3

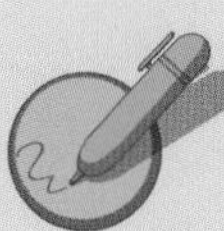

23 Look and write.

1 
2 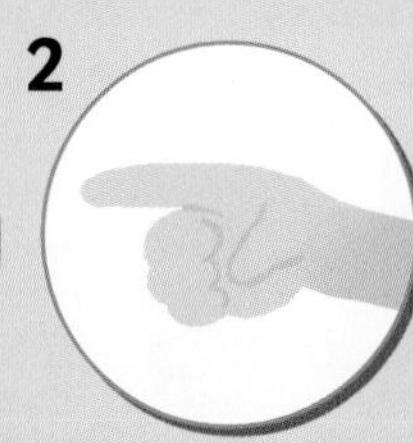
3 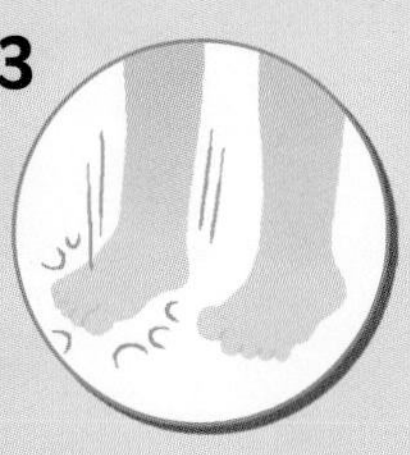
4 
5 
6 

1 ______________ your toes!

2 ______________ your fingers!

3 ______________ your feet!

4 ______________ your hands!

5 ______________ your head!

6 ______________ your body!

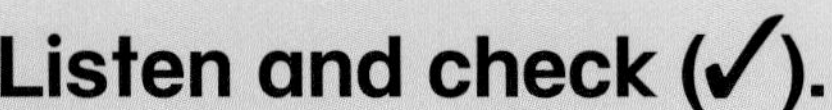

24 Listen and check (✓).

A:78

1 a 
b 

2 a 
b 

3 a 
b 

4 a 
b 

I can talk about exercise and movement. ☐

I can show how to exercise. ☐

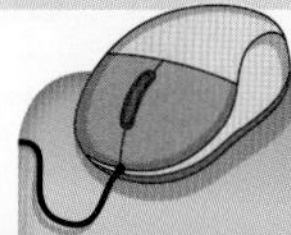

Now go to Tropical Island.

4 My face

1 B:02 Listen.

2 B:03 Listen and say.

3 B:04 Listen and number.

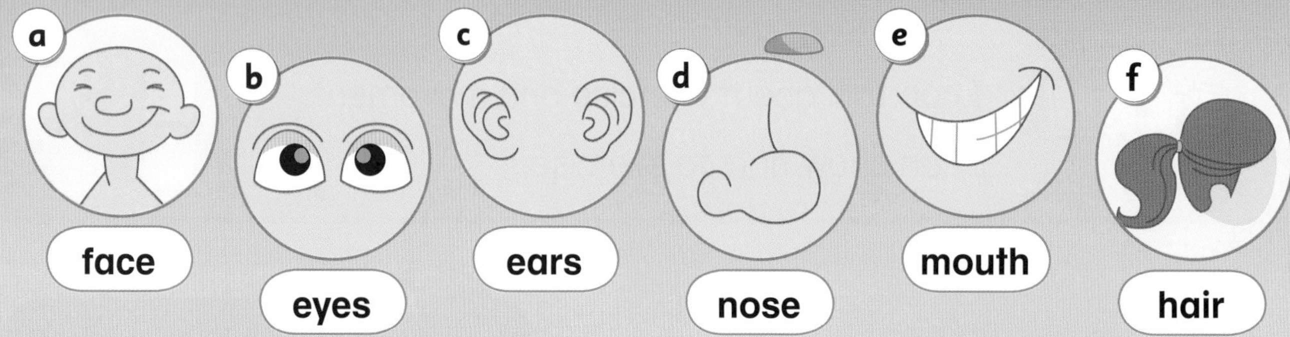

4 B:05-06 Listen and chant. (See page 109.)

B:07 LOOK!

I have a small nose.	He/She has a small nose.
Do you have a small nose?	Yes, I do. / No, I don't.
Does he/she have a small nose?	Yes, he/she does. / No, he/she doesn't.

5 B:08 Listen and draw. Then draw yourself and say.

girl

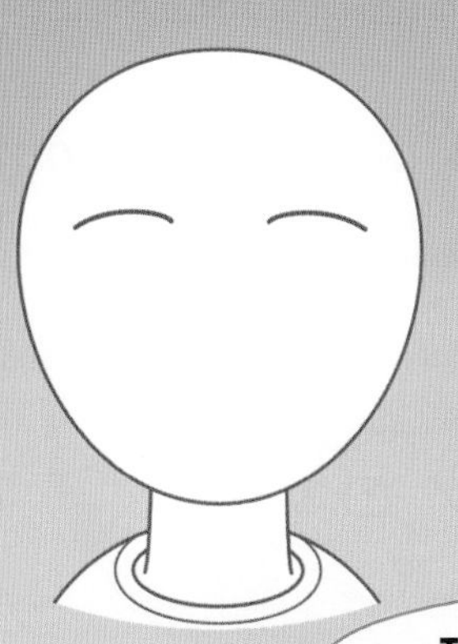

me

I have big eyes.

6  Stick. Then listen and say.

a  long

b short

c  curly

d  straight

e  dark

f  blond

g   neat

h  messy

 7  Listen and write. Then sing.

Who is it? Who can it be?
Who is it? Listen to me!

She has blue eyes, blue eyes,
And a small nose, a small nose.
She has small ears, small ears,
And __________, __________ hair.
Who is it? It's Susie!

Who is it? Who can it be?
Who is it? Listen to me!

He has brown eyes, brown eyes,
And a small nose, a small nose.
He has a big mouth, a big mouth,
And __________, __________ hair.
Who is it? It's Tommy.

Who is it? Who can it be?
Who is it? Listen to me!

She has green eyes, green eyes,
And a big nose, a big nose.
She has big ears, big ears,
And __________, __________ hair.
Who is it? It's Mary!

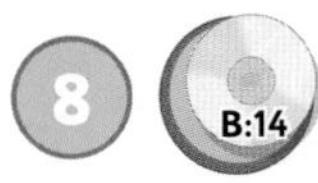

Listen and number. Then say.

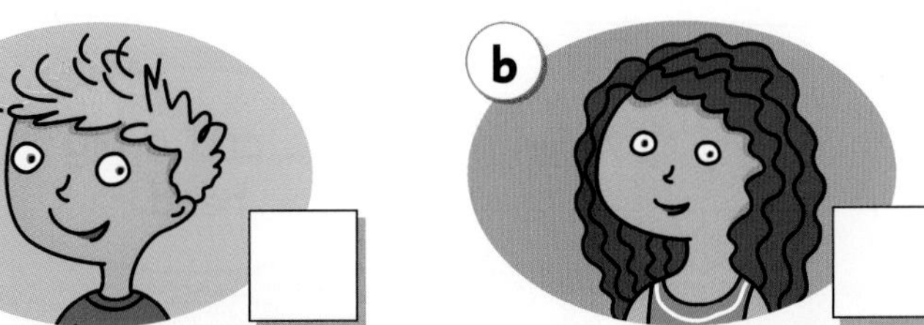

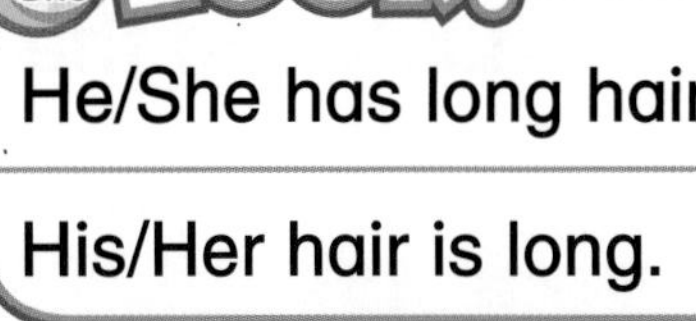

He/She has long hair.

His/Her hair is long.

He has messy hair. His nose is small.

Look, write, and circle.

Grandpa

Emma

Tom

Aunt Jane

1 Who is it?

It's ________________. (His / Her) hair is straight and blond.

2 Who is it?

It's ________________. (His / Her) hair is dark and curly.

3 Who is it?

It's ________________. (His / Her) hair is short and curly.

4 Who is it?

It's ________________. (His / Her) hair is short and straight.

  Listen to the story.

11 Circle.

1 Pippin's eyes are (big / small).

2 Pippin's head is (big / small).

3 Pippin's mouth is (big / small).

4 Pippin's nose is (big / small).

5 Pippin is (yellow and green / red and blue).

6 Pippin is (Lindy's / Emily's) friend.

12 Role-play the story.

13 Complete for yourself. Then ask a friend.

	eyes	nose	ear	hair
Me				
My friend				

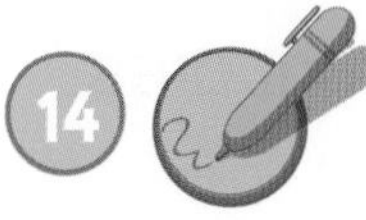

14 Write about yourself.

I have ______________________________

______________________________________.

HOME-SCHOOL LINK

Talk to your family about respecting differences.

15 Listen and point. Then say.

1 circle

2 triangle

3 square

4 rectangle

5

16 Count and write.

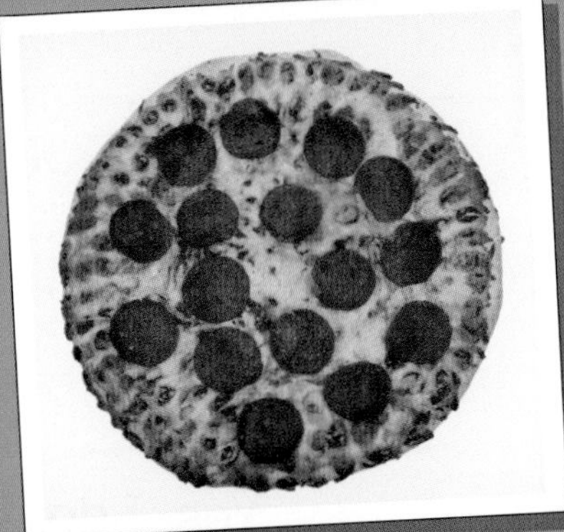

______ circles

______ triangle

______ squares

______ rectangles

______ triangles

______ squares

______ rectangle

______ circle

MINI-PROJECT

Make a picture with different shapes, sizes, and colors.

  **Listen.**

1 **ai**

2  **ee**

  **Listen, point, and say.**

19  **Listen and blend the sounds.**

1 t - ai - l tail
2 r - ai - n rain
3 m - ai - l mail
4 w - ai - t wait
5 s - ee see
6 f - ee - t feet
7 w - ee - k week
8 sh - ee - p sheep

20  **Underline *ai* and *ee*. Read the words aloud.**

1 feet

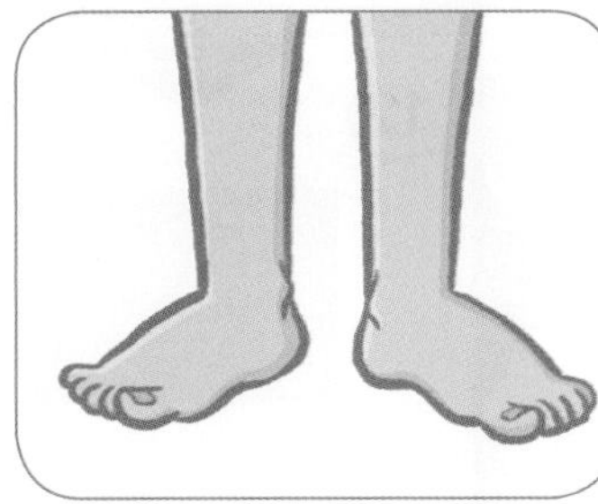

2 rain

3 mail

4 sheep

5 tail

6 week

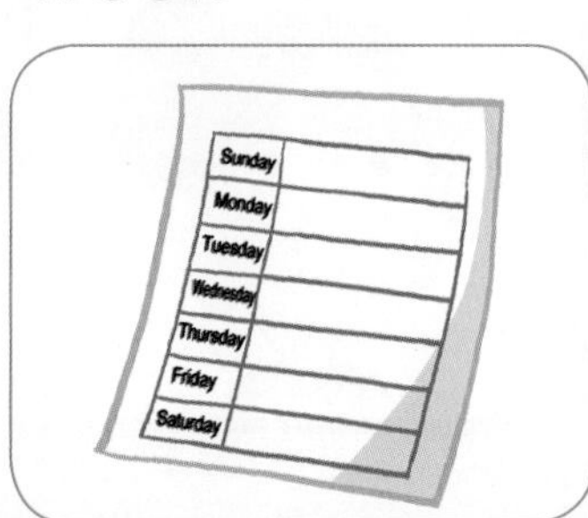

21 **Listen. Then play.**

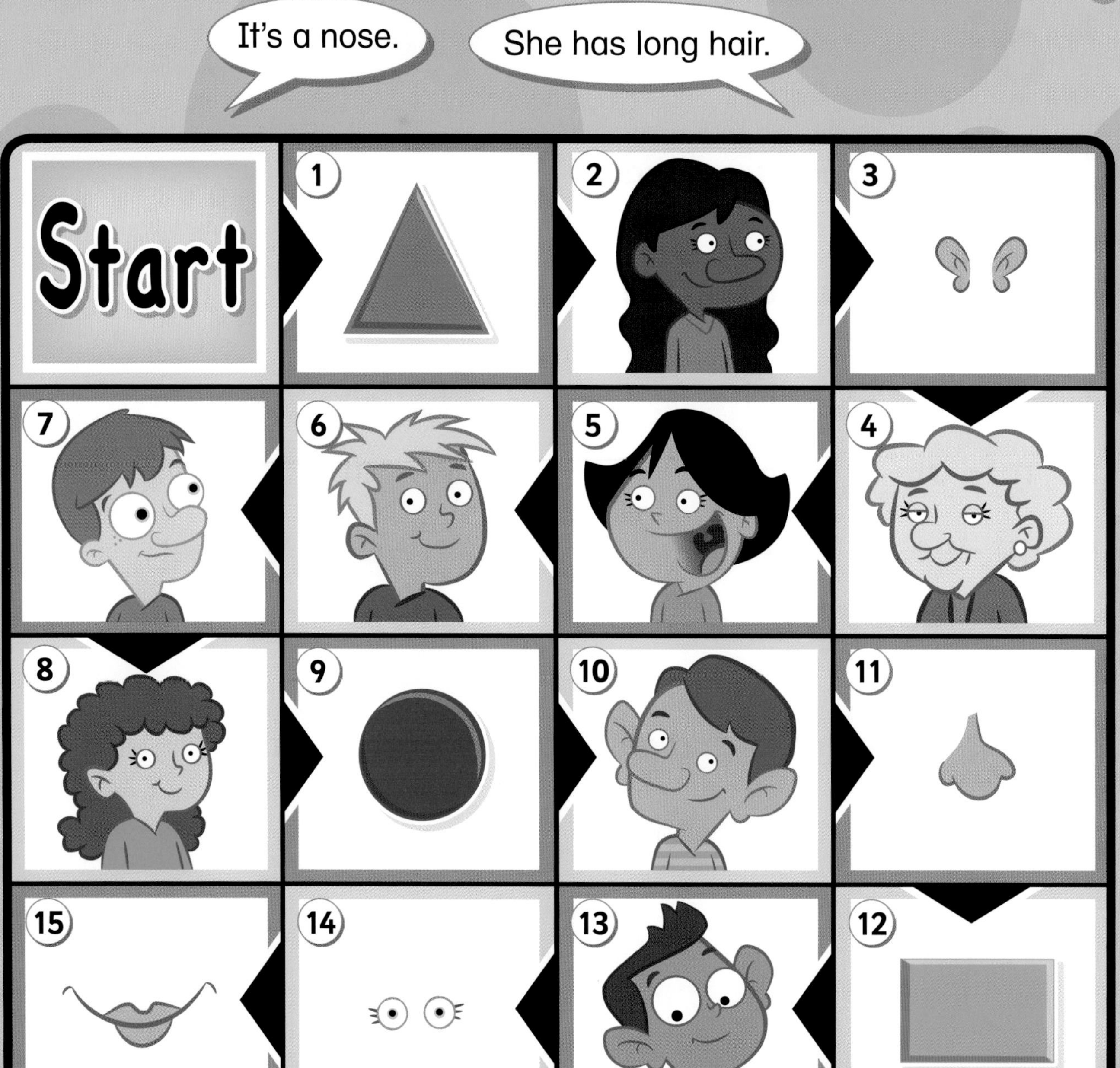

It's a nose.

She has long hair.

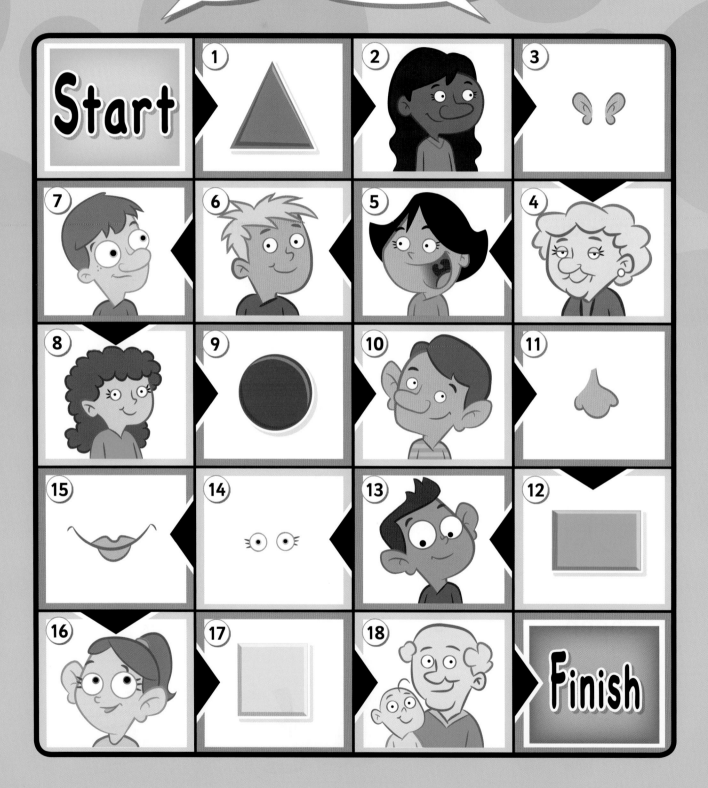

Start	1	2	3
7	6	5	4
8	9	10	11
15	14	13	12
16	17	18	Finish

22 **Listen and move.**

  Listen and check (✓).

1 a b

2 a b

3 a b

4 a b

5 a b

6 a b

7 a b

8 a b

I can talk about faces.

I can name and find shapes.

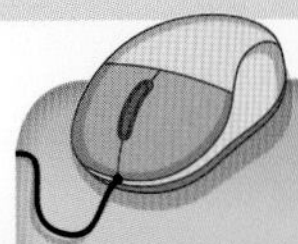

Now go to Tropical Island.

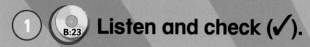

Review Units 3 and 4

1 Listen and check (✓).

B:23

1 a

b

2 a

b

3 a

b

4 a

b

5 a

b

6 a

b

2 Write.

1

She can ______________
______________________.

2

He ______________
______________________.

3

He ______________
______________________.

4

She ______________
______________________.

5

He ______________
______________________.

6

She ______________
______________________.

3 Listen and draw.

1

boy

2

girl

4 Listen and write.

Simon

Ann

Bob

Sally

1 Who is it? It's Ann.

2 Who is it? ____________________

3 Who is it? ____________________

4 Who is it? ____________________

5 Who is it? ____________________

5 Animals

1 B:26 Listen.

2 B:27 Listen and say.

3 B:28 Listen and number.

a

cow

b

goat

c

chicken

d

turkey

e

duck

f

sheep

g

horse

4 B:29-30 Listen and chant. (See page 109.)
B:31 LOOK!
What's this/that?
It has big eyes.
It's black and white. It's a cow.
5 B:32 Listen and number. Then ask and answer.
a
b
c
d
What's this?
It has long legs.
It's black and white.
It's a cow.
B:33
Quest

6 B:34 Stick. Then listen and say.

VOCABULARY

a bat
b crow
c skunk
d owl
e fox

TIP!
one fox
two foxes

Stick

7 B:35-36 Listen and write. Then sing.

SONG

Chorus:
I'm Max. And I'm Maisie.
We're animal crazy!

What's this?
What's this?
It's small and green.
It has big eyes.
It's a ____________!

(Chorus)

What are these?
What are these?
They're black and white.
They have a tail.
They're ____________!

(Chorus)

What's that?
What's that?
It's small and gray.
It has two wings.
It's a ____________!

(Chorus)

What are those?
What are those?
They're thin and black.
They have two legs.
They're ____________!

(Chorus)

LOOK!

B:37

Is it small?	Is it a bat?	Yes, it is. / No, it isn't.
Are the bats big?		Yes, they are. / No, they aren't.

8 B:38 **Listen and write. Then ask and answer.**

1

____

2

____

3

____

4

____

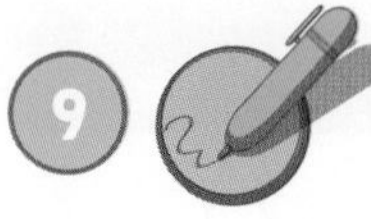

9 **Draw. Then ask and answer.**

Is it a/an …?

Are the …?

Listen to the story.

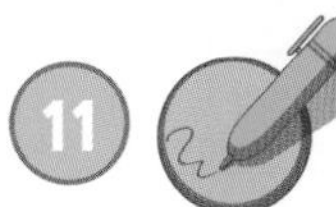

11 Match. Then circle the animal in the story.

12 Role-play the story.

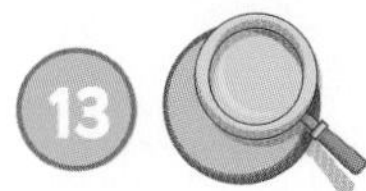

13 Show how animals help us. Look and stick.

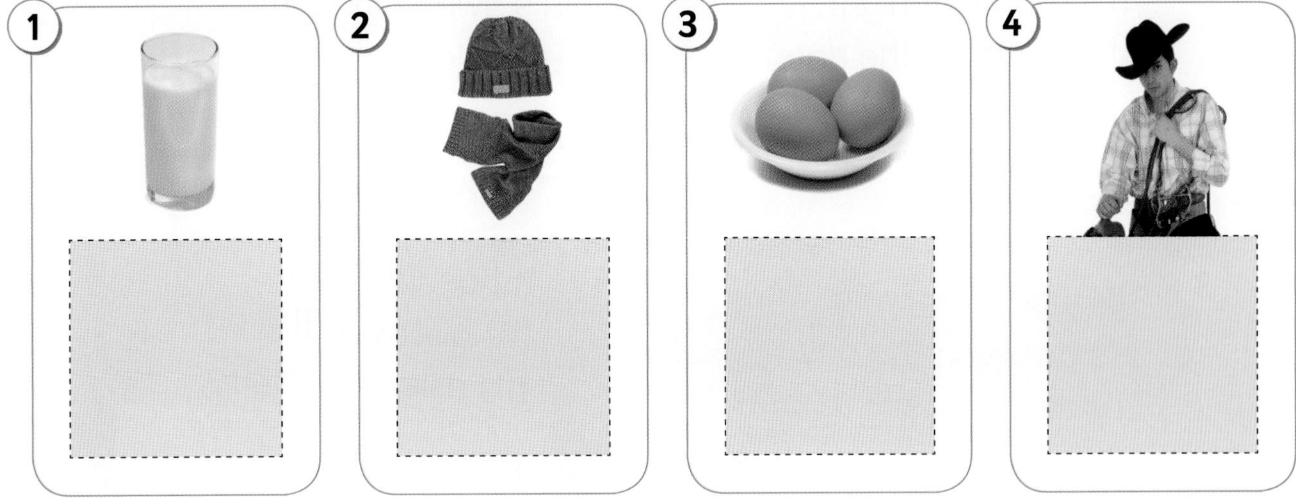

HOME-SCHOOL LINK

Describe your favorite animal to your family.
Talk about its colors and what it looks like.

14 Listen and point. Then say.

15 Read and find. Then write.

1 It's brown.
It's awake at night.
It's asleep in the day.
It's a ______________.

2 It has two legs and a big head.
It's awake at night.
It's asleep in the day.
It's an ______________.

3 It's black and white.
It's awake in the day.
It's asleep at night.
It's a ______________.

4 It has two legs.
It's awake in the day.
It's asleep at night.
It's a ______________.

16 Choose an animal. Describe it.

17  **Listen.**

1 **igh**

2 **oa**

18 B:42 **Listen, point, and say.**

19 B:43 **Listen and blend the sounds.**

1 h - igh high

2 s - igh sigh

3 l - igh - t light

4 r - igh - t right

5 b - oa - t boat

6 c - oa - t coat

7 s - oa - p soap

8 g - oa - t goat

20 **Underline *igh* and *oa*. Read the words aloud.**

1 boat

2 high

3 goat

4 light

5 soap

6 coat

21 B:44 **Listen. Then play.**

HAVE FUN!

22 B:45 **Listen and act.**

23 Listen and number.

a 

b 

c 

d 

e 

f 

24 Listen and check (✓).

1 a  b 

2 a  b 

3 a  b 

4 a  b 

I can talk about what animals look like. ☐

I can talk about how animals help us. ☐

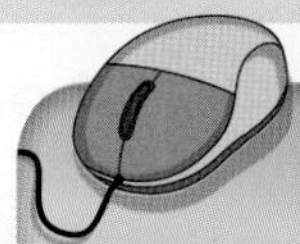

Now go to Tropical Island.

6 Food

1 B:48 Listen.

2 B:49 Listen and say.

3 B:50 Listen and number.

a pizza

b chicken

c fish

d rice

e eggs

f burgers

g hot dogs

h apples

i bananas

4 B:51-52 **Listen and chant.** (See page 109.)

B:53 **LOOK!**

What's your favorite food?	My favorite food is pizza.
I like chicken.	I don't like fish.

B:54 Quest

5 Look and write. Then draw and say.

1

I like ____________.

2

I don't like ____________.

3

I ____________________.

4

I ____________________.

My favorite food

I like ____________

____________________.

6 B:55 Listen and say.

VOCABULARY

a pineapple
b coconut
c pumpkin
d corn
e toast
f cereal
g grapes
h beans
i raisins
j nuts

7 B:56-57 Listen and write. Then sing.

SONG

Chorus:

I eat breakfast, I eat lunch, I eat dinner. How about you?
I eat breakfast, I eat lunch, I eat dinner. How about you?

I like ____________ and ____________, too.
I like ____________. How about you?
I like ____________. My favorite dish!
But I don't like ____________!

(Chorus)

I like ____________ and ____________, too.
I like ____________. How about you?
I like ____________. It's very nice,
But I don't like ____________!

(Chorus)

B:58 LOOK!

He/She	likes / doesn't like	pineapple for breakfast.
Does he/she like pineapple for breakfast?	Yes, he/she does. / No, he/she doesn't.	

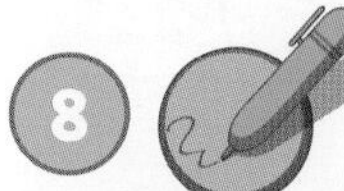

8 Look and circle. Then ask and answer.

1

She (likes / doesn't like) toast for breakfast.

2

Does he like grapes for breakfast?
(Yes, he does. / No, he doesn't.)

3

Does he like corn for lunch?
(Yes, he does. / No, he doesn't.)

Does she like toast for breakfast?

Yes, she does.

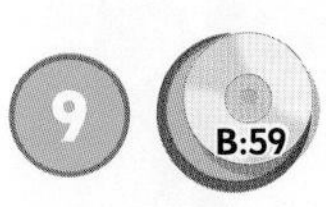

9 Listen and stick. Then say.

1

2

Stick

She likes cereal for breakfast.

Listen to the story.

1

Happy birthday, Princess Emily ....

2

An apple?

Huh! I don't like apples!

3

Fish?

I don't like fish.

I like fish.

4

I don't like pizza ....

I like pizza!

5

I don't like cake!!

6

I like parrots. Where's my parrot?

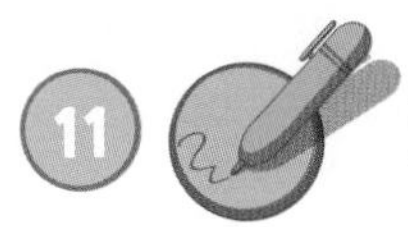

11 Read and check (✓).

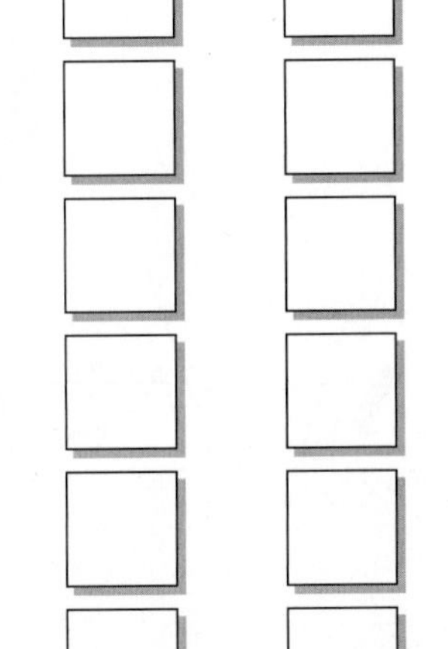

		YES	NO
1	It is Princess Emily's birthday.		
2	Princess Emily is happy.		
3	Princess Emily likes apples.		
4	Princess Emily doesn't like fish.		
5	Princess Emily likes pizza.		
6	Princess Emily doesn't like cake.		
7	Princess Emily likes Pippin.		

12 Role-play the story.

13 Look and circle the good food and snacks.

HOME-SCHOOL LINK

Talk about healthy snacks at home.

PARENT

 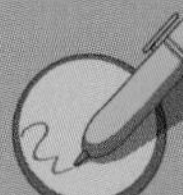 Read, look, and match. Then say.

1

2

3

a I like eggs, tortillas, and juice for breakfast.

b I like noodles, vegetables, and tea for breakfast.

c I like croissants, yogurt, and coffee for breakfast.

 Complete for yourself. Then ask a friend and write.

What's your favorite food?

I like chicken and salad for dinner.

	NAME	DINNER
1	Me	
2	Friend	chicken and salad
3		
4		
5		

 Show and tell a friend.

My friend likes chicken and salad for dinner.

MINI-PROJECT
Draw your favorite lunch or dinner.

17 B:61 **Listen.**

1 **oo**

2 oo

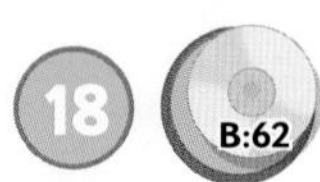

18 B:62 **Listen, point, and say.**

19 B:63 **Listen and blend the sounds.**

1	z - **oo**	zoo		2	t - **oo**	too
3	f - **oo** - d	food		4	m - **oo** - n	moon
5	b - oo - k	book		6	f - oo - t	foot
7	l - oo - k	look		8	c - oo - k	cook

20 **Underline *oo*. Read the words aloud.**

1 moon

2 cook

3 zoo

4 foot

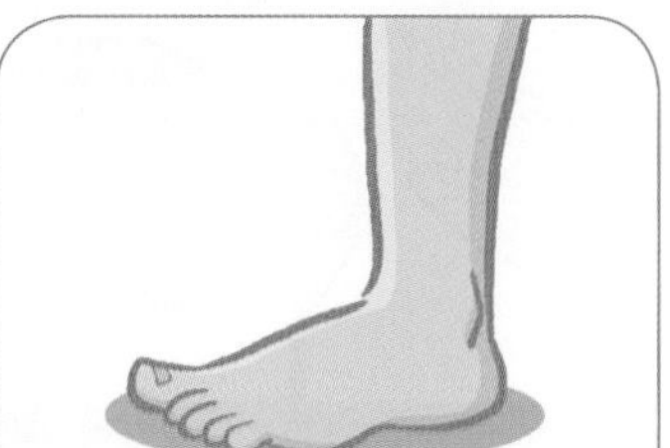

5 book

6 food

  **Listen. Then play.**

I like fish for dinner.

I don't like toast for breakfast.

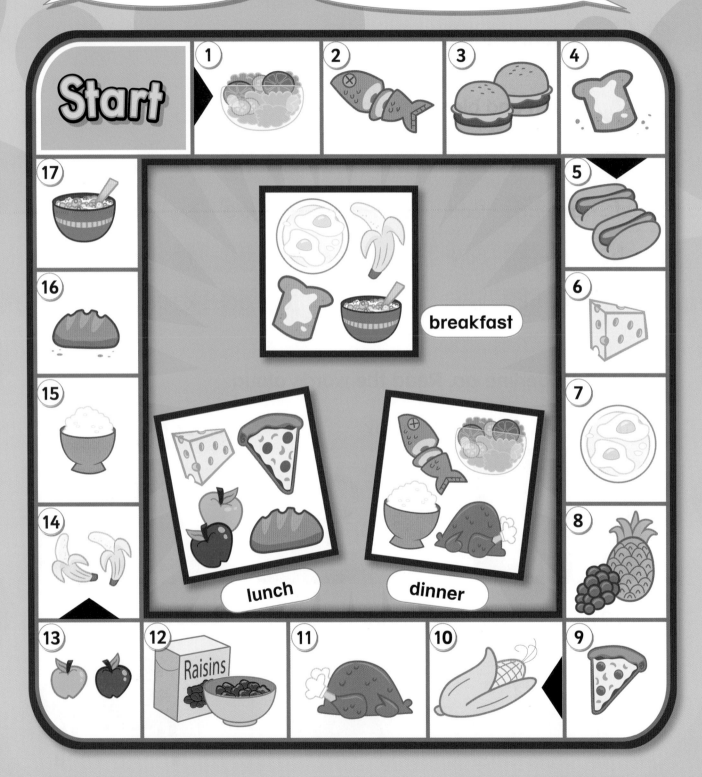

Start

1 2 3 4 5 6 7 8 9 10 11 12 13 14 15 16 17

breakfast

lunch

dinner

Raisins

  **Listen and move.**

6

Listen and check (✓).

1 a

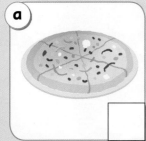

b 

2 a 

b 

3 a

b 

4 a 

b 

5 a 

b 

6 a 

b 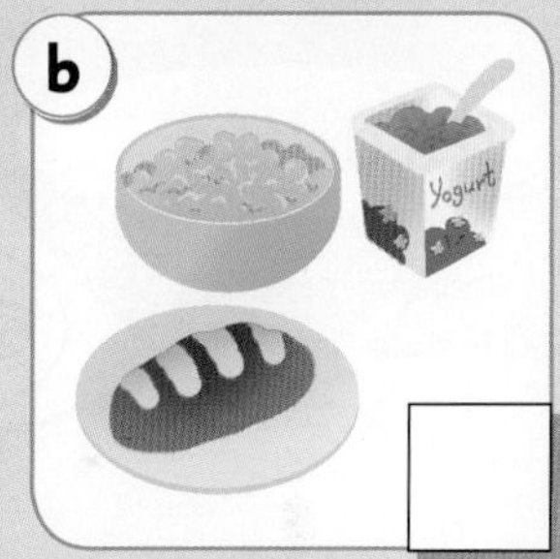

7 a 

b 

8 a 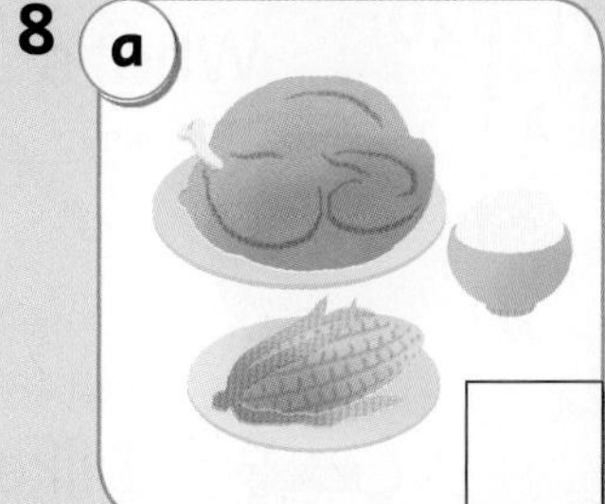

b 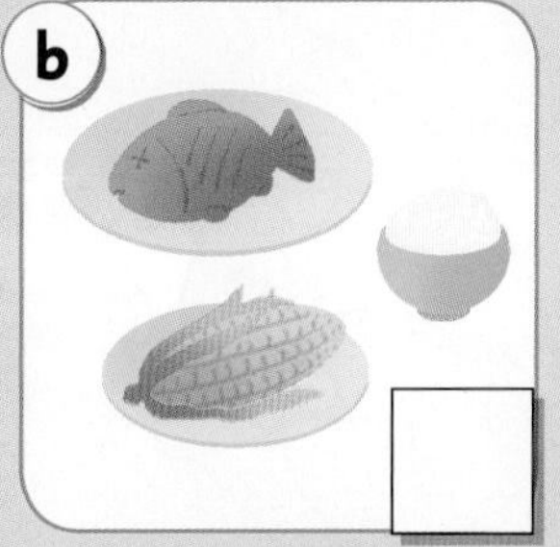

I can talk about food. ☐

I can say what I like and don't like. ☐

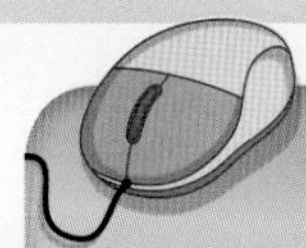

Now go to Tropical Island.

Review Units 5 and 6

1 B:67 **Listen. Then play.**

4
...?
No, I don't.
5
...
3
It has ....
8
... for dinner.
7
Is it a chicken?
6
... for dinner.
14
... for breakfast.
NUTS
RAISINS
15
It's asleep ....
16
...
18
...?
Yes, he does.
17
...?
Yes, they are.
24
It's a ....
25
Is it a horse?
Finish

7 Clothes

1 C:02 Listen.

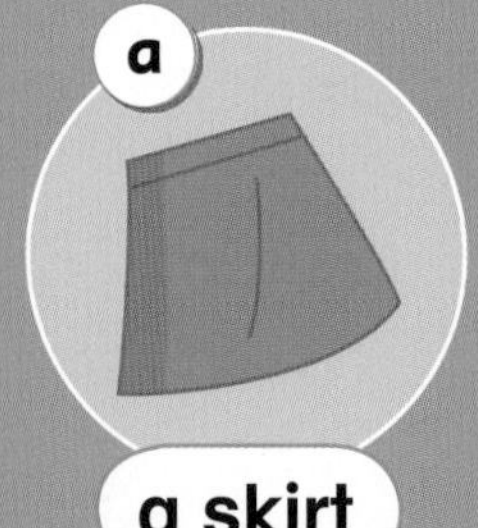

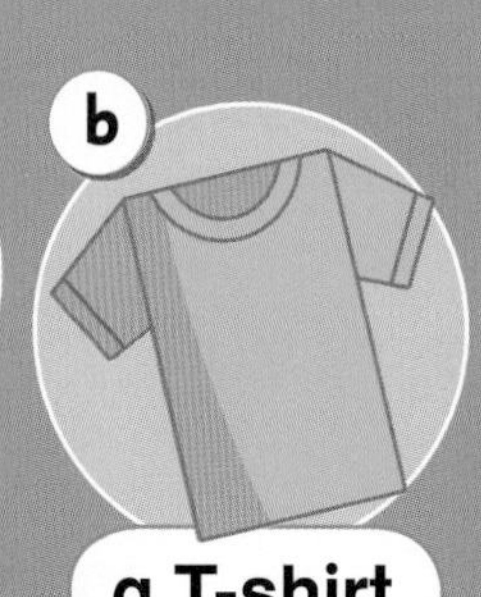

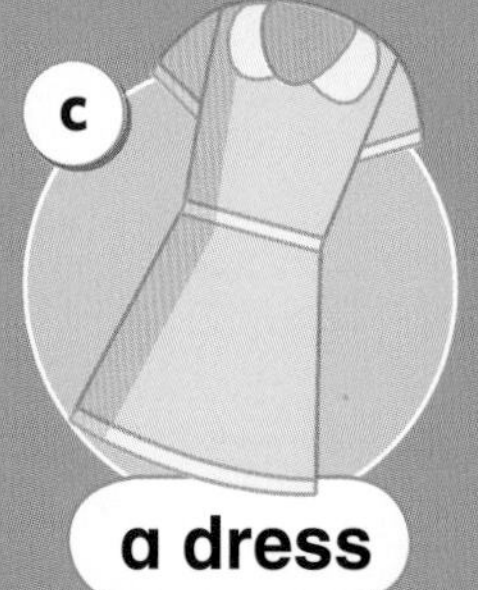

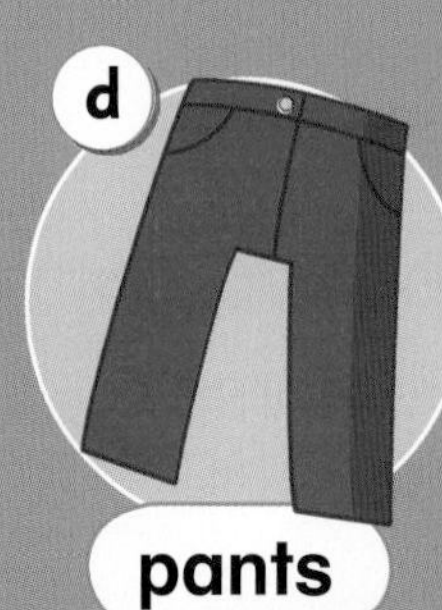

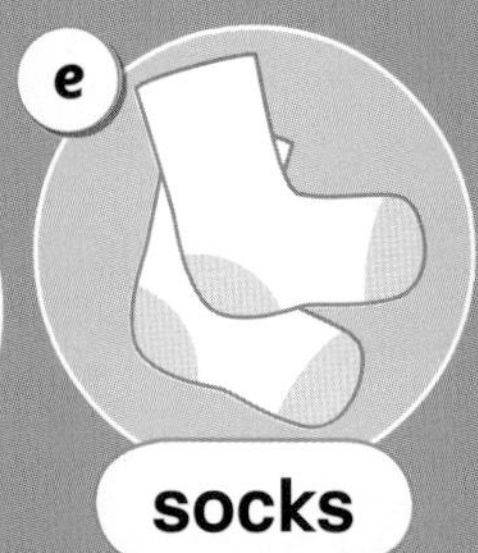

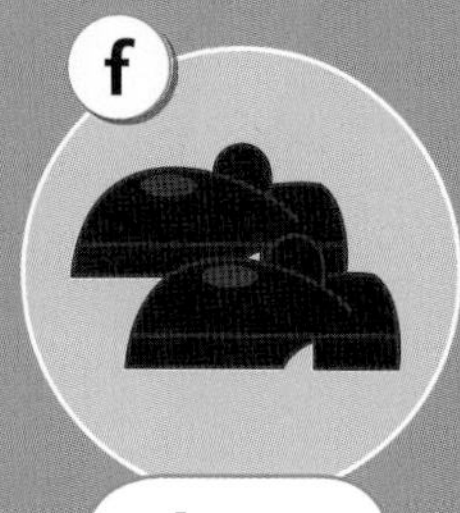

4 C:05-06 Listen and chant. (See page 110.)
C:07 LOOK!
I'm wearing a white skirt.
I'm not wearing white pants.
5 C:08 Listen and color. Then say.
1
2
3
I'm wearing a yellow dress and red shoes.
C:09
Quest

6 C:10 **Listen and say.**

VOCABULARY

7 C:11-12 **Listen and write. Then sing.**

SONG

Good morning!
Good morning!
Take off your ______________.
It's time for school!

Put on your ______________.
Put on your ______________.
Put on your ______________.
Off you go!
It's time for school!

Good night!
Good night!
Put on your ______________.
It's time for bed!

Take off your ______________.
Take off your ______________.
Take off your ______________.
Off you go!
It's time for bed.

Good night! Good night!
Good night! Good night!

What do you want?	I want a shirt, please.
Do you want a blue shirt?	Yes, I do. / No, I don't. I want a red shirt.

8 C:14 **Listen and circle. Then ask and answer.**

1

2

3

What do you want?

I want boots, please.

Do you want brown boots?

No, I don't. I want red boots.

9 **Stick. Then ask and answer.**

Do you want a black T-shirt?

No, I don't. I want a white T-shirt.

10 Listen to the story.

1
It's the palace! We're here!
Stop! Do you have a shoe?

2
What? I have two shoes. Look!
And I'm wearing two shoes, too.

3
No! Do you have this shoe?
Oh ...

4
Ow!!!

5
My shoe! Thank you!

6
My parrot! Pippin!
Awk! Hello, Princess!

11 Read, look, and match.

1 I'm wearing brown shoes and a brown shirt.

2 I'm wearing a pink dress and one pink shoe!

3 I'm wearing blue pants and orange shoes.

4 We're wearing hats. They're blue, black, and yellow.

12 Role-play the story.

13 Look and stick.

HOME-SCHOOL LINK

Make a list of polite words. Use them at home with your family.

  Listen and point. Then say.

15 C:17 Listen and number.

MINI-PROJECT Make a poster to describe your school uniform or the uniform of someone doing a job.

  **Listen.**

1 ar 2 ir 3 or 4 ur

  **Listen, point, and say.**

 **Listen and blend the sounds.**

1 c - ar car
2 sh - ar - k shark
3 s - ir sir
4 g - ir - l girl
5 f - or for
6 c - or - n corn
7 f - ur fur
8 s - ur - f surf

 **Underline *ar, ir, or,* and *ur*. Read the words aloud.**

1 shark

2 corn

3 girl

4 surf

5 car

6 fur

HAVE FUN!

Listen. Then play.

Put on your T-shirt.

Take off your shoes.

Start

1

2

3 Go forward two spaces.

4

5

6

7 Go forward one space.

8

9

10 Go back one space.

11

12

a

b

c

Listen and act.

PROGRESS CHECK

Listen and match.

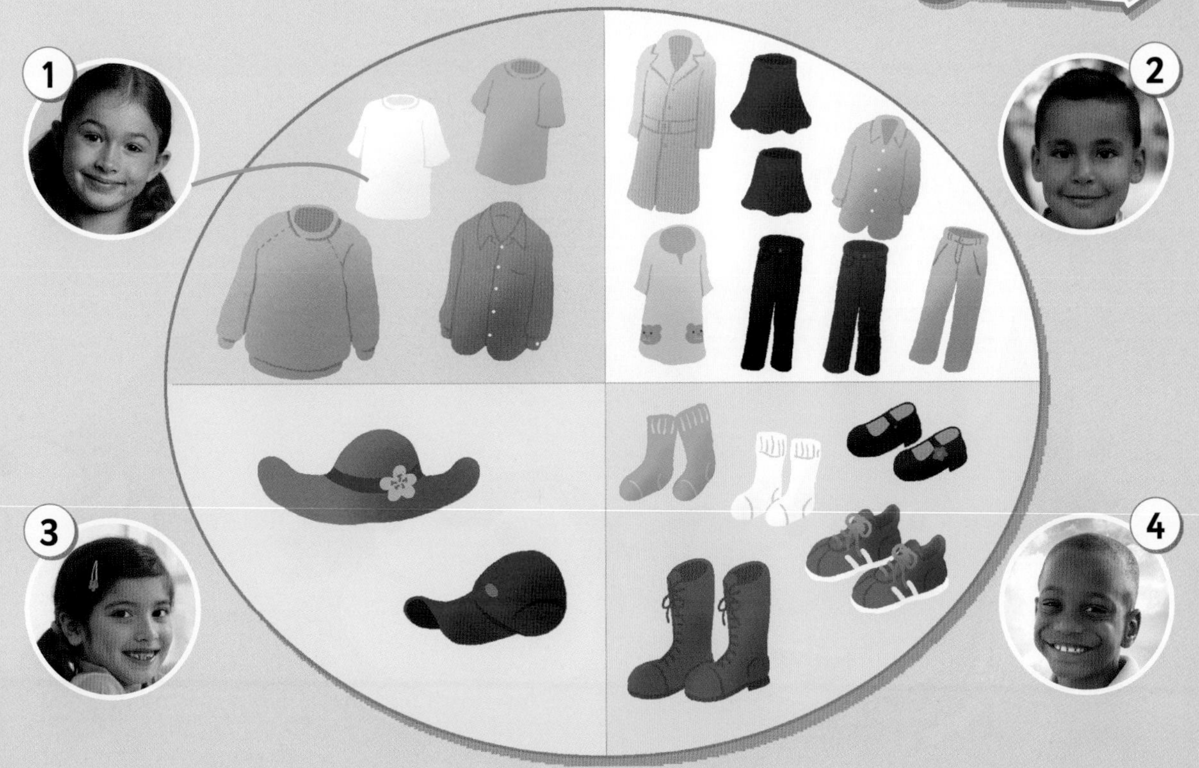

Listen and check (✓).

1 

2 

3 

4 

I can talk about my clothes. ☐

I can describe uniforms. ☐

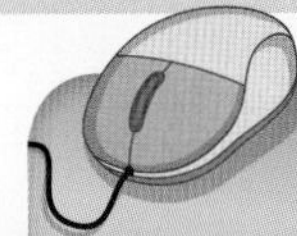

Now go to Tropical Island.

8 Weather

1 C:25 Listen.
WELCOME
2 C:26 Listen and say.
3 C:27 Listen and number.
a cloudy
b snowy
c rainy
d windy
e sunny
f cool

4 Listen and chant. (See page 110.)

C:28-29

LOOK! C:30

Do you like cloudy days?	Yes, I do. / No, I don't.
I like cloudy days.	I don't like cloudy days.

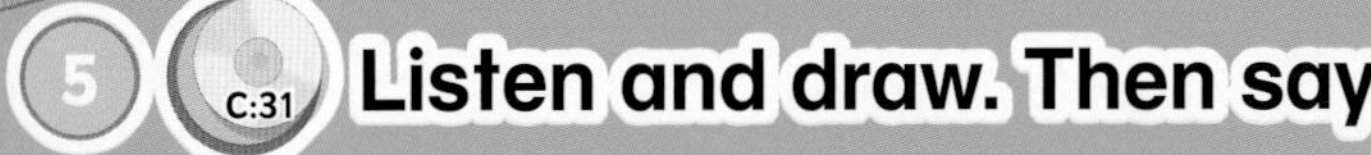

5 Listen and draw. Then say.

C:31

I don't like windy days.

1 

2 

3 

4 

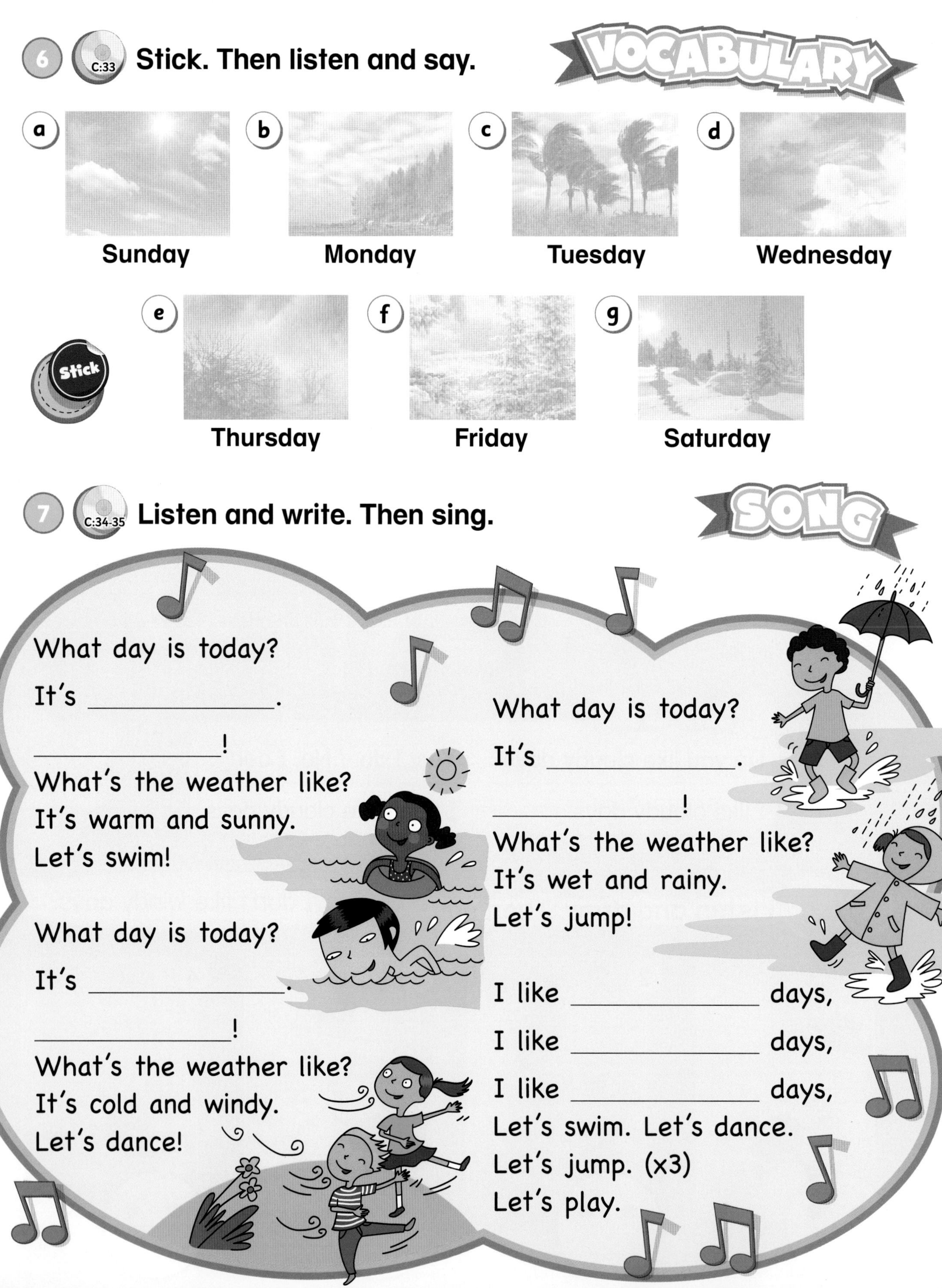

6 Stick. Then listen and say.

C:33

VOCABULARY

a Sunday

b Monday

c Tuesday

d Wednesday

e Thursday

f Friday

g Saturday

Stick

7 Listen and write. Then sing.

C:34-35

SONG

What day is today?
It's ____________.
____________!
What's the weather like?
It's warm and sunny.
Let's swim!

What day is today?
It's ____________.
____________!
What's the weather like?
It's cold and windy.
Let's dance!

What day is today?
It's ____________.
____________!
What's the weather like?
It's wet and rainy.
Let's jump!

I like ____________ days,
I like ____________ days,
I like ____________ days,
Let's swim. Let's dance.
Let's jump. (x3)
Let's play.

What day is today?	It's Sunday.
What's the weather like?	It's sunny.

8 C:37 Listen, circle, and draw. Then ask and answer.

1 Sunday Monday Tuesday Wednesday Thursday Friday Saturday

It's windy.
It's cool.
It's sunny.

2 Sunday Monday Tuesday Wednesday Thursday Friday Saturday

It's cloudy.
It's sunny.
It's windy.

3 Sunday Monday Tuesday Wednesday Thursday Friday Saturday

It's snowy.
It's rainy.
It's cool.

What day is today?
It's Tuesday.
What's the weather like?
It's sunny.

 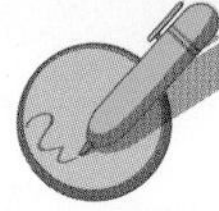

9 Write about yourself. Then ask your friends.

What day is today? It's ______________.

What's the weather like? It's ______________.

Do you like ______________ days?

Friends' names	
	I like ______________ days.
	I don't like ______________ days.

Listen to the story.

1

Oh Pippin ....

Awk! Emily!!

2

Oh. I'm sorry! Thank you. My name's Princess Emily.

Wow! You're the princess!

3

Yes, I am! But I don't like my crown. I like your clothes.

Oh!

4

But Pippin's my friend.

My new friends— Joe and Lindy.

5

New friends. Oh! Are you hungry?

Yes, we are!

6

WELCOME HOME, PIPPIN!

Now I have three friends.

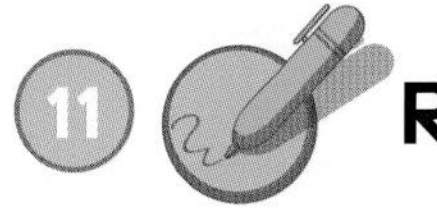

11 Read and circle.

1 What's the weather like? It's cloudy. / It's rainy.

2 Is Princess Emily happy? Yes, she is. / No, she isn't.

3 Does Princess Emily like her crown? Yes, she does. / No, she doesn't.

4 Does Princess Emily like Lindy's clothes?

Yes, she does. / No, she doesn't.

5 How many friends does Princess Emily have now?

one friend / three friends

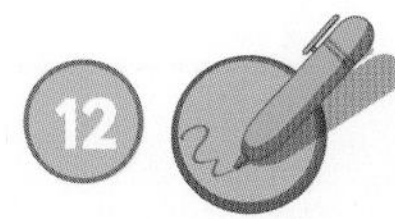

12 What does Emily learn to share in the story? Circle.

13 Role-play the story.

Share with friends and family.

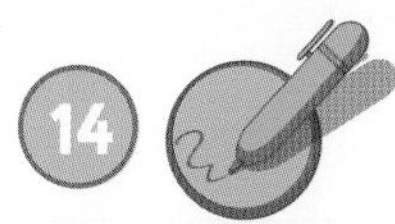

14 Circle what you can share.

a 

b 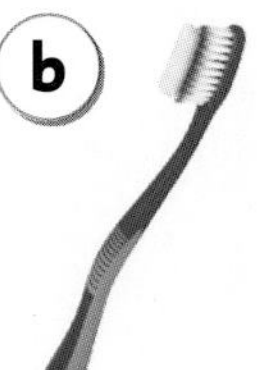

c 

d

e 

f 

g 

Make or draw a good-to-share list.
Show your family.

15 Listen and point. Then write and say.

1 freezing

2 cold

3 warm

4 hot

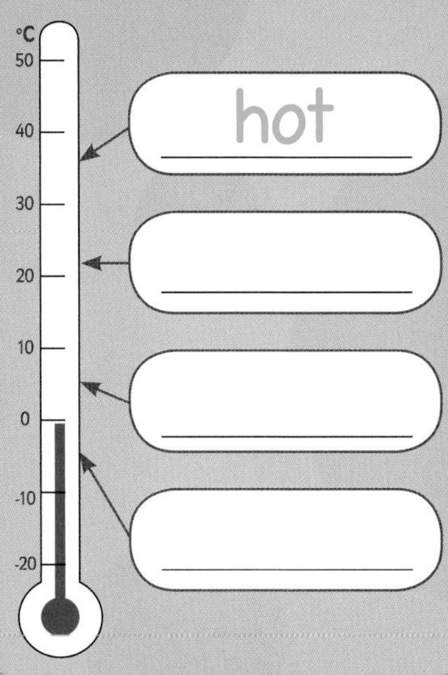

16 Listen and write.

1 It's ______________.
It's sunny.

2 It's ______________.
It's windy.

3 It's ______________.
It's cloudy.

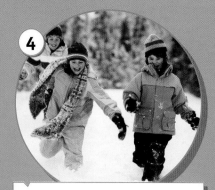

4 It's ______________.
It's snowy.

5 It's ______________.
It's rainy.

17 C:41 Listen.

1 **ow**

2 **oy**

18 C:42 Listen, point, and say.

19 C:43 Listen and blend the sounds.

1	ow - l	owl	2	n - ow	now
3	c - ow	cow	4	d - ow - n	down
5	b - oy	boy	6	t - oy	toy
7	j - oy	joy	8	c - ow - b - oy	cowboy

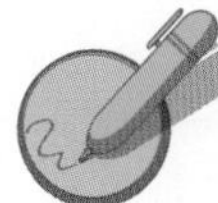

20 Underline *ow* and *oy*. Read the words aloud.

1 boy

2 owl

3 toy

4 cow

5 cowboy

6 down

  Listen. Then play.

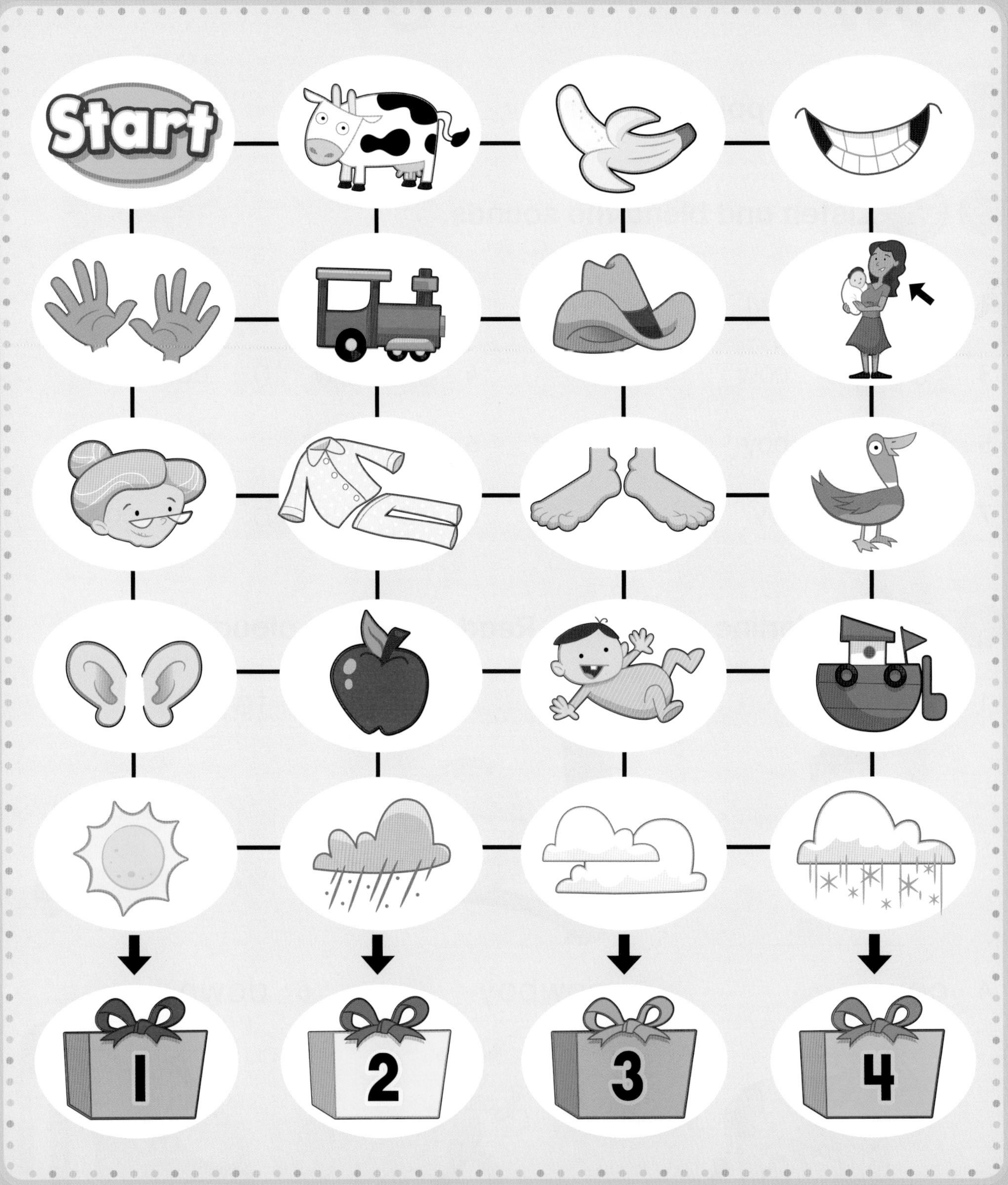

Start

1 2 3 4

  Listen and act.

Listen and check (✓).

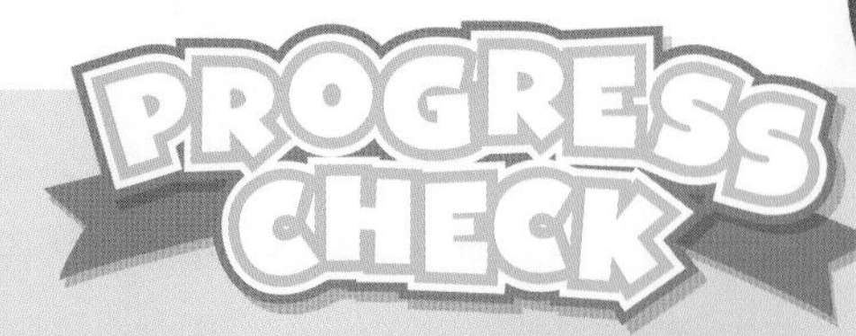

1

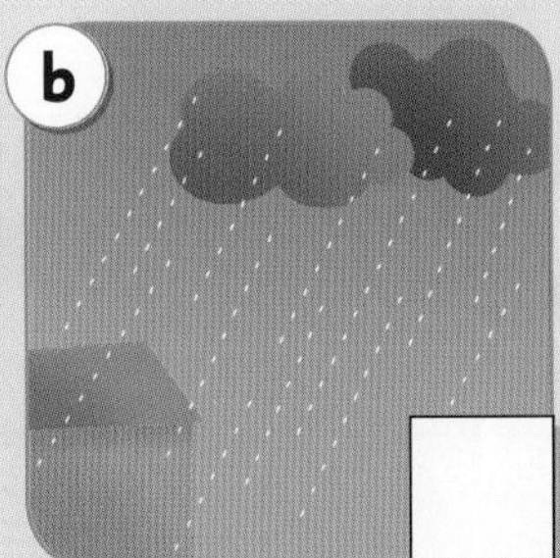

2
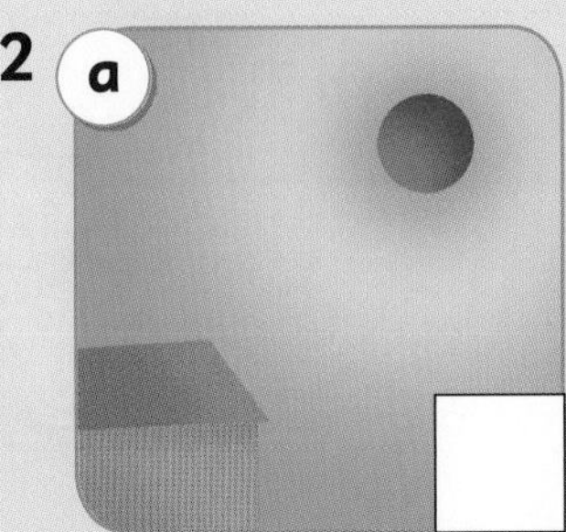

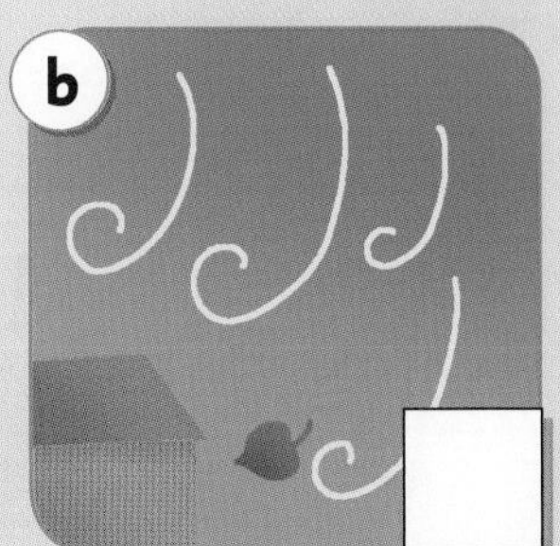

3

4

5

6

7

8

I can talk about the weather and temperatures. ☐

I can read temperature on a thermometer. ☐

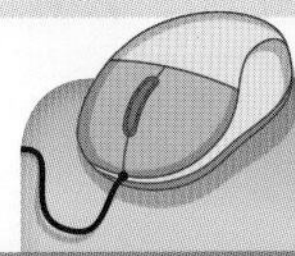

Now go to Tropical Island.

Review Units 7 and 8

1 C:47 **Listen. Then play.**

3
Move
...?
CALENDAR
S M T W T F S
4
It's Wednesday.
5
...?
It's cloudy.
6
...?
Yes, I do.
7
Move
8
I'm
wearing ....
CALENDAR
S M T W T F S
14
What day is today?
...
15
I'm
wearing ....
16
...
17
Move
...?
No, I don't.
CALENDAR
S M T W T F S
24
What day
is today?
...
25
What's the
weather like?
...
Finish

Goodbye

1 C:48 Listen, find, and circle.

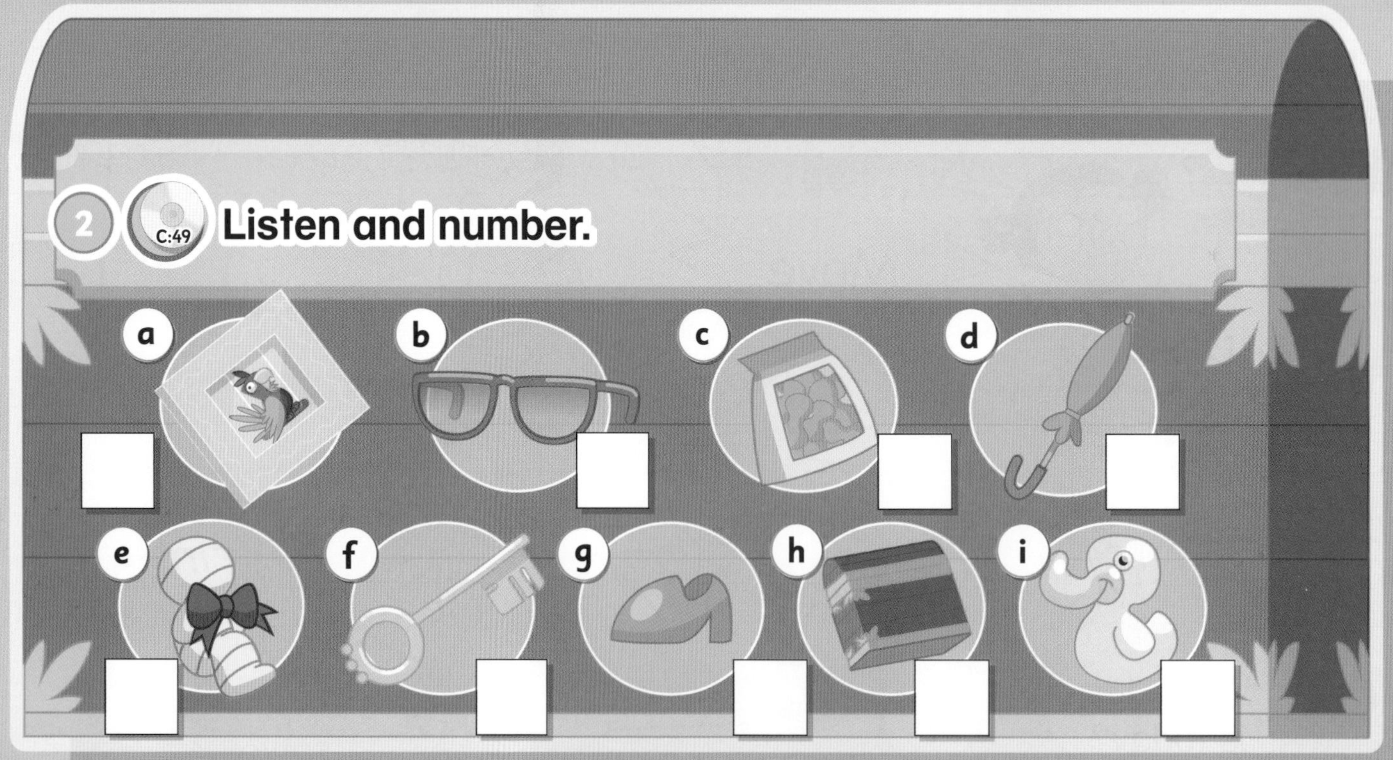

2 C:49 Listen and number.

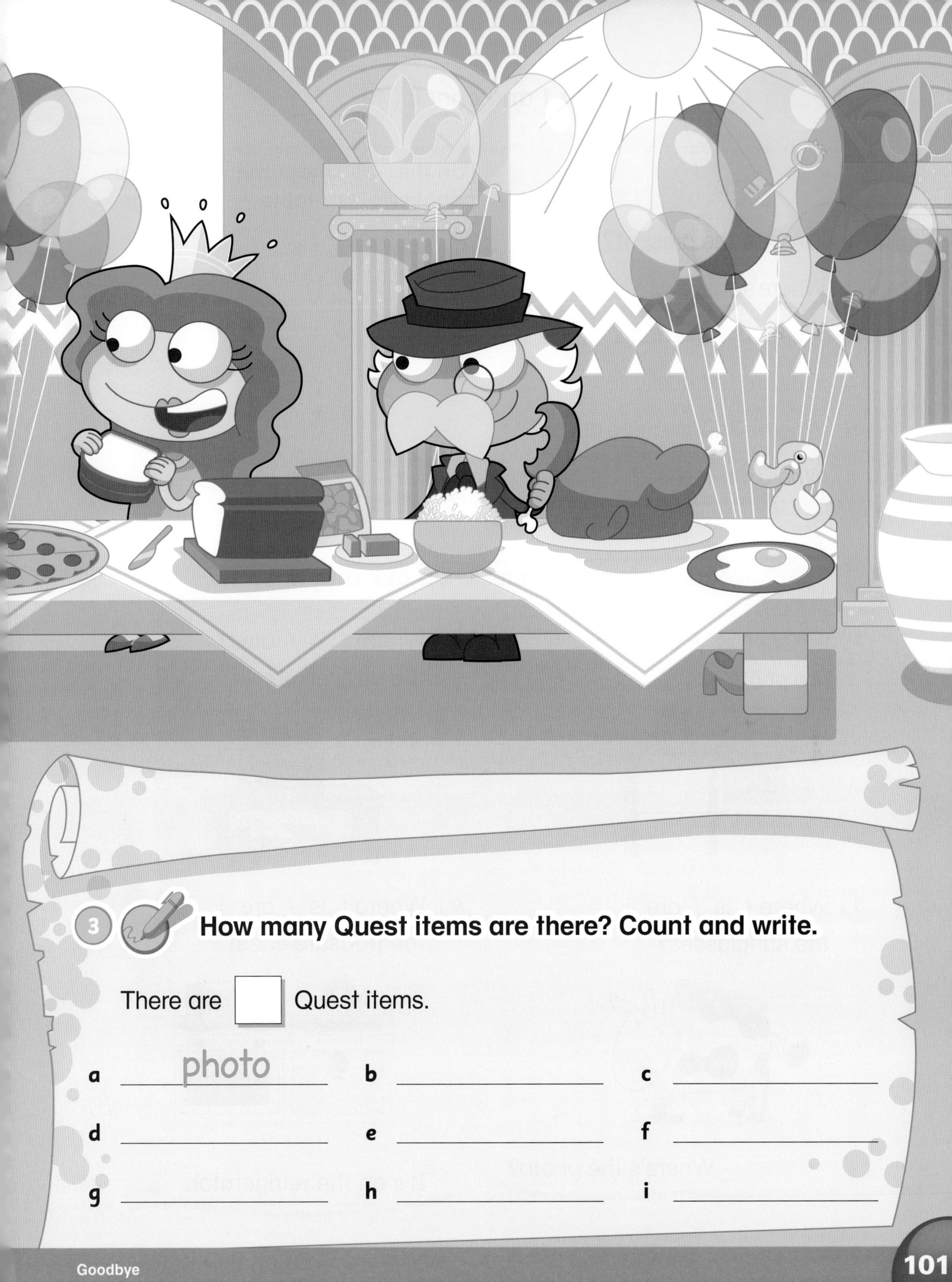

3 How many Quest items are there? Count and write.

There are ☐ Quest items.

a photo
b
c
d
e
f
g
h
i

 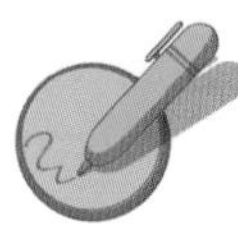

Look at Activity 1 and check (✓).

	on the table	under the table	in the cage
1 Where's the present?		✓	
2 Where's the photo?			
3 Where are the nuts?			
4 Where's the duck?			
5 Where's the treasure chest?			
6 Where's the shoe?			

 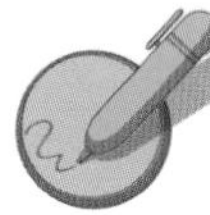

Read, look, and circle. Then ask and answer.

1 Where (is / are) the photo?

2 Where (is / are) the umbrellas?

3 Where (is / are) the sunglasses?

4 Where (is / are) the treasure chest?

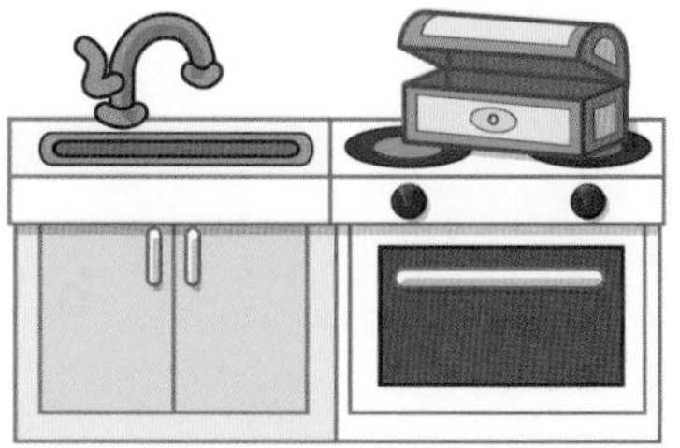

Where's the photo?

It's on the refrigerator.

6 C:50-51 **Listen and sing.**

SONG

Stand up, jump up, come on a quest,
Come on a quest today.
Turn around, sit down, come on a quest,
Come on a quest today.
A treasure chest, a present, a photo, a key,
sunglasses, a duck, nuts, a shoe, and an umbrella.
We have them all today.

Princess Emily has new friends,
And Pippin's home again – Hooray!
Princess Emily has new friends,
And Pippin's home again – Hooray!
Hooray! Hooray! Hooray!
Hooray! Hooray! Hooray!

7 **Draw five of your favorite things. Then show and tell.**

Easter

1 C:52-53 **Make. Then listen and sing.** (See page 110.)

2 **Play the game.**

rabbit

egg

chick

flower

1

1		
2		
3		

2

1		
2		
3		

Christmas

1 C:54-55 **Listen and sing. Then find and say.** (See page 110.)

star

Christmas tree

stocking

Santa

present

2  **Make and play.**

Valentine's Day

1 C:56-57 **Listen and sing. Then find and say.** (See page 111.)

2 **Make and say.**

Halloween

1 C:58-59 **Listen and sing. Then find and say.** (See page 111.)

candy

jack-o'-lantern

witch

2 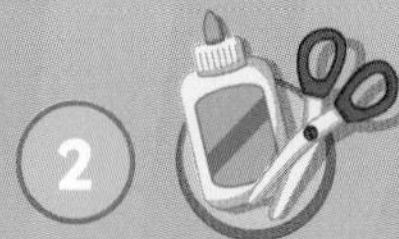 **Prepare. Then have a party.**

Welcome

4 A:04 .... page 7

Paint a rainbow in the sky.
Red, orange, yellow.
Red, orange, yellow.
Red, orange, yellow.
Red, orange, yellow.
Red, orange, yellow.

Paint a rainbow in the sky.
Purple, blue, green, pink.
Purple, blue, green, pink.
Purple, blue, green, pink.
Purple, blue, green, pink.
Purple, blue, green, pink.

A:05 .... Karaoke version

Unit 1 My toys

4 A:19 .... page 13

What's this? It's red.
It's a car!
What's that? It's blue.
It's a boat!
What are these? They're pink.
They're dolls!
What are those? They're green.
They're trains!
What's this? It's orange.
It's a ball!
What's that? It's yellow.
It's a bike!
What are these? They're purple.
They're kites!
What are those? They're brown.
They're teddy bears!

A:20 .... Karaoke version

Unit 2 My family

4 A:39 .... page 23

Who's he?
He's my brother.
Who's she?
She's my sister.
Who's he?
He's my grandpa.
They're my family. Hey, hey!

Who's he?
He's my uncle.
Who's she?
She's my aunt.
Who's he?
He's my cousin.
They're my family. Hey, hey!

A:40 .... Karaoke version

Unit 3 Move your body

4 A:61 .... page 35

Arms, arms, wave your arms,
Wave your arms with me.
Feet, feet, stamp your feet,
Stamp your feet with me.
Hands, hands, clap your hands,
Clap your hands with me.
Toes, toes, touch your toes,
Touch your toes with me.
Legs, legs, move your legs,
Move your legs with me.
Body, body, shake your body,
Shake your body with me.

Stamp, stamp, stamp.
Move, wave, shake.
Clap, clap, clap!

A:62 .... Karaoke version

Unit 4 **My face**

4 B:05 .... page 45

Princess. Look!
I have small eyes.
I have a big nose.
I have a small mouth.
And I have short hair.
Short, short hair.
Short, short hair.
Argh!

I have big eyes.
I have a small nose.
I have a big mouth.
And I have long hair.
Long, long hair.
Long, long hair.
Ah!

Unit 5 **Animals**

What's this? Is it a sheep?
No, it's a goat.
Is it white?
No, it's brown.
Is it fat?
No, it's thin!

What's that? Is it a chicken?
No, it's a duck.
Is it big?
No, it's small.
Is it red?
No, it's white.

What's this? Is it a turkey?
No, it's a cow.
Is it small?
No, it's big.
Is it yellow?
No, it's black and white.

What are those? Are they sheep?
Yes, they are!
Mah, quack, moo, baa!
Mah, quack, moo, baa!
Mah, quack, moo, baa!
Mah, quack, moo, baa!

Unit 6 **Food**

What's your favorite food?
What's your favorite food?
I like apples.
I like bananas.
But I don't like eggs or burgers. Hey!

What's your favorite food?
What's your favorite food?
I like chicken.
I like fish.
But I don't like pizza or rice. Hey!

B:52 .... Karaoke version

Unit 7 Clothes

4 C:05 .... page 79

I'm wearing red pants.
Red pants, red pants.
I'm wearing red pants.
How about you?

I'm wearing a purple skirt.
A purple skirt, a purple skirt.
I'm wearing a purple skirt.
How about you?

I'm not wearing green shoes.
Green shoes, green shoes.
I'm not wearing green shoes.
They're brown, brown, brown.

I'm not wearing pink socks.
Pink socks, pink socks.
I'm not wearing pink socks.
They're white, white, white!

C:06 .... Karaoke version

Unit 8 Weather

4 C:28 .... page 89

Do you like sunny days?
Do you like sunny days?
Yes, I do. Yes, I do.
I like sunny days.

Do you like rainy days?
Do you like rainy days?
No, I don't. No I don't.
I don't like rainy days.

Do you like snowy days?
Do you like snowy days?
Yes, I do. Yes, I do.
I like snowy days.

Do you like windy days?
Do you like windy days?
No, I don't. No, I don't.
I don't like windy days.

C:29 .... Karaoke version

Easter

1 C:52 .... page 104

Hello, Easter Bunny.
How are you today?
Wake up, wake up,
Come and play.

Jump, jump, jump,
Easter Bunny, jump!
Turn around, turn around,
Fall down with a thump.

Hello, Easter Bunny.
How are you today?
Wake up, wake up,
Come and play.

Jump, jump, jump,
Easter Bunny, jump!
Turn around, turn around,
Fall down with a thump.

Christmas

1 C:54 .... page 105

Hang up your stockings
By the Christmas tree.
Hang up your stockings,
It's Christmas Eve.
It's Christmas Eve.

Who's this with a brown sack
In the living room?
With a long white beard
And a big red nose
And he laughs with a ho, ho, ho!

Is it true? Can it be?
Yes, it's Santa! Come and see.
With a long white beard
And a big red nose
And presents for you and me.

Hang up your stockings
By the Christmas tree.
Hang up your stockings,
It's Christmas Eve.
It's Christmas Eve.

C:55 .... Karaoke version

Valentine's Day

1 C:56 .... page 106

I'm so happy!
Let's sing and play.
I'm so happy!
It's Valentine's Day!

Here's a flower for my mom.
Some chocolates for my dad.
Here's a heart for Grandma,
And a card for Grandpa.

I'm so happy!
Let's sing and play.
I'm so happy!
It's Valentine's Day!

C:57 .... Karaoke version

Halloween

1 C:58 .... page 107

Come on! It is Halloween!
It's time to trick-or-treat!
The moon is smiling up there
And the stars are out there.
Do you have some yummy candy ready for me?
Are you a ghost or a scary witch?
Jack-o'-lanterns smile at me!

Come on! It is Halloween!
It's time to trick-or-treat!
The moon is smiling up there
And the stars are out there.
Do you have some yummy candy ready for me?
Are you a ghost or a scary witch?
Jack-o'-lanterns smile at me!

C:59 .... Karaoke version

Picture dictionary

Numbers

sixteen

seventeen

eighteen

nineteen

twenty

Days of the week

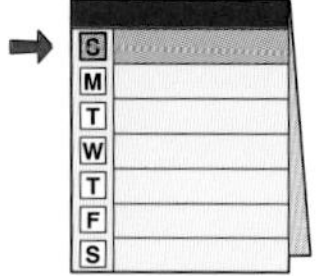

Sunday

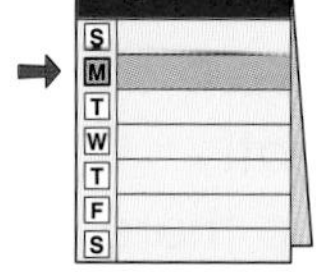

Monday

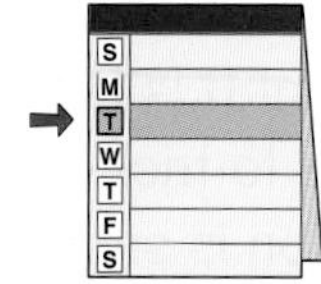

Tuesday

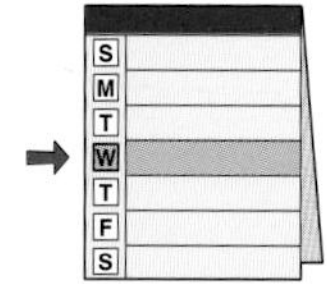

Wednesday

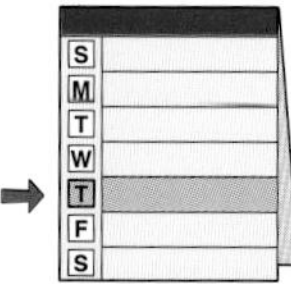

Thursday

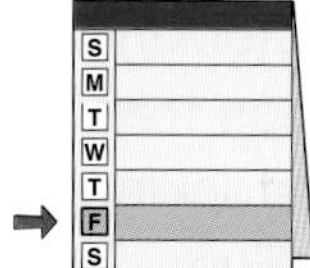

Friday

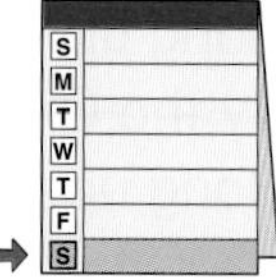

Saturday

Time

one o'clock

two o'clock

three o'clock

four o'clock

five o'clock

six o'clock

seven o'clock

eight o'clock

nine o'clock

ten o'clock

eleven o'clock

twelve o'clock

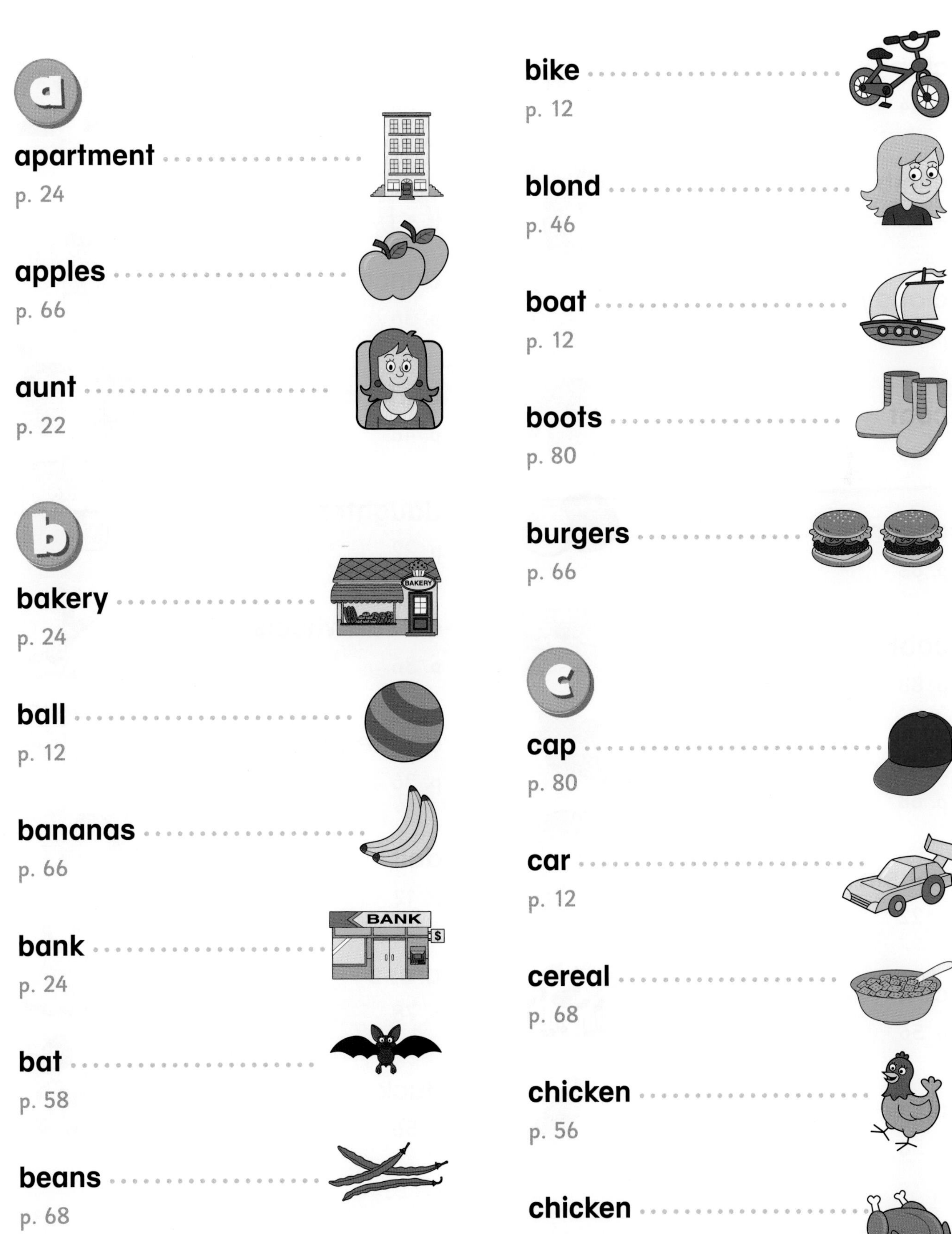

a

apartment
p. 24

apples
p. 66

aunt
p. 22

b

bakery
p. 24

ball
p. 12

bananas
p. 66

bank
p. 24

bat
p. 58

beans
p. 68

bike
p. 12

blond
p. 46

boat
p. 12

boots
p. 80

burgers
p. 66

c

cap
p. 80

car
p. 12

cereal
p. 68

chicken
p. 56

chicken
p. 66

clap
p. 34

climb
p. 36

cloudy
p. 88

coat
p. 80

coconut
p. 68

cool
p. 88

corn
p. 68

cousin
p. 22

cow
p. 56

crow
p. 58

curly
p. 46

d

dance
p. 36

dark
p. 46

daughter
p. 22

do cartwheels
p. 36

do the splits
p. 36

doll
p. 12

dress
p. 78

duck
p. 56

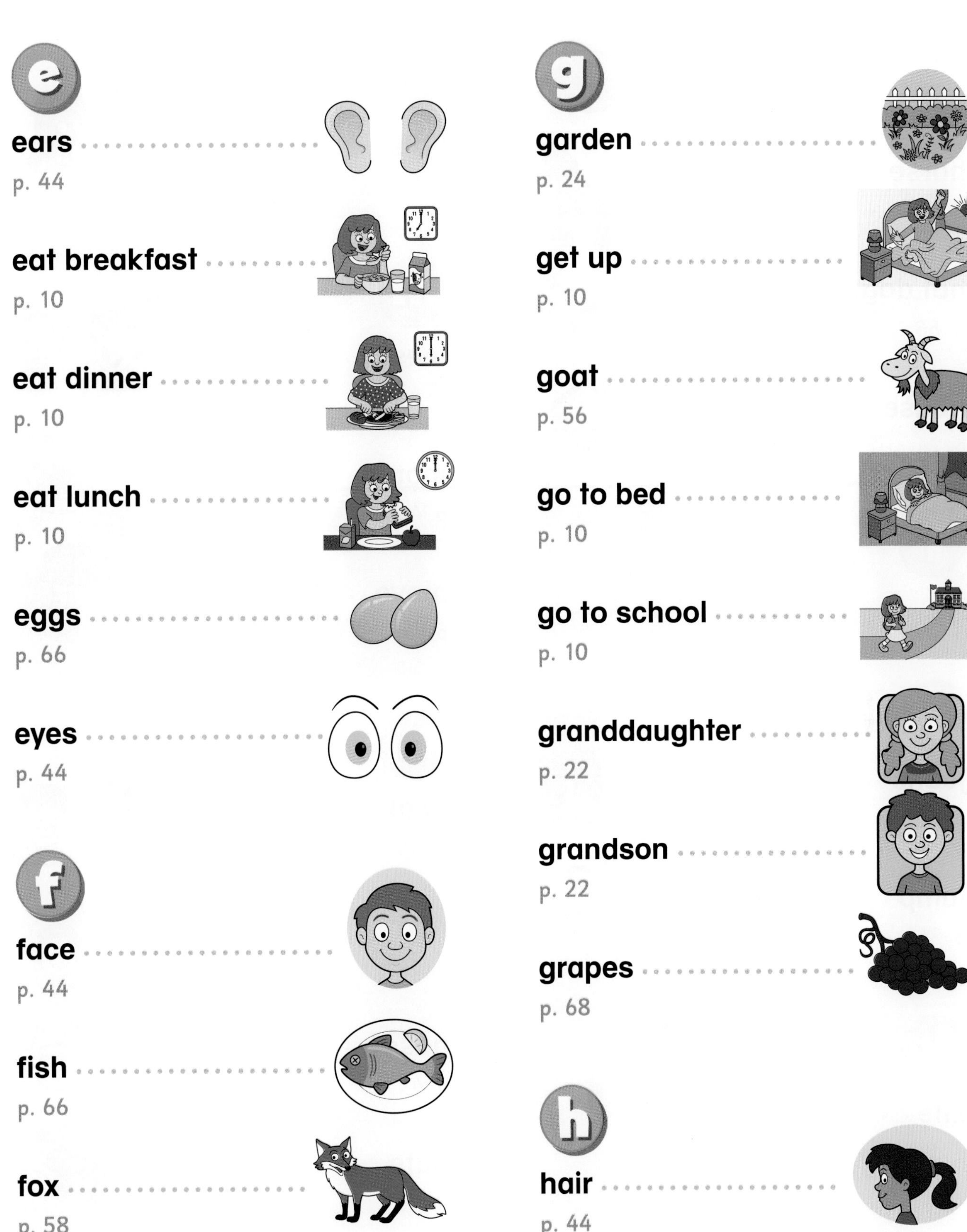

e

ears
p. 44

eat breakfast
p. 10

eat dinner
p. 10

eat lunch
p. 10

eggs
p. 66

eyes
p. 44

f

face
p. 44

fish
p. 66

fox
p. 58

g

garden
p. 24

get up
p. 10

goat
p. 56

go to bed
p. 10

go to school
p. 10

granddaughter
p. 22

grandson
p. 22

grapes
p. 68

h

hair
p. 44

hat p. 80

horse p. 56

hot dogs p. 66

house p. 24

i

j

jeans p. 80

jump p. 36

k

kite p. 12

l

long p. 46

m

messy p. 46

mouth p. 44

move p. 34

n

neat p. 46

nod p. 34

nose p. 44

nuts p. 68

owl p. 58

pajamas p. 80

pants p. 78

pineapple p. 68

pizza p. 66

point p. 34

post office p. 24

pumpkin p. 68

rainy p. 88

raisins p. 68

restaurant p. 24

rice p. 66

shake p. 34

sheep p. 56

shirt p. 80

shoes p. 78

short p. 46

skirt
p. 78

skunk
p. 58

sneakers
p. 80

snowy
p. 88

socks
p. 78

son
p. 22

stamp
p. 34

stand on your head
p. 36

store
p. 24

straight
p. 46

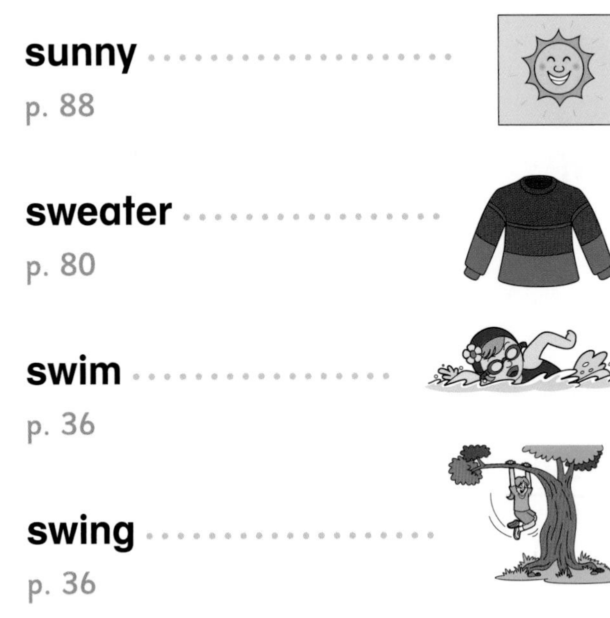

sunny
p. 88

sweater
p. 80

swim
p. 36

swing
p. 36

teddy bear
p. 12

toast
p. 68

touch
p. 34

train
p. 12

T-shirt
p. 78

turkey
p. 56

uncle
p. 22

wake up
p. 10

wave
p. 34

windy
p. 88

Acknowledgments

The Publishers would like to thank the following teachers for their suggestions and comments on this course:

Asako Abe
JiEun Ahn
Nubia Isabel Albarracín
José Antonio Aranda Fuentes
Juritza Ardila
María del Carmen Ávila Tapia
Ernestina Baena
Marisela Bautista
Carmen Bautista
Norma Verónica Blanco
Suzette Bradford
Rose Brisbane
María Ernestina Bueno Rodríguez
María del Rosario Camargo Gómez
Maira Cantillo
Betsabé Cárdenas
María Cristina Castañeda
Carol Chen
Carrie Chen
Alice Chio
Tina Cho
Vicky Chung
Marcela Correa
Rosalinda Ponce de Leon
Betty Deng
Rhiannon Doherty
Esther Domínguez
Elizabeth Domínguez
Ren Dongmei
Gerardo Fernández
Catherine Gillis
Lois Gu
SoRa Han
Michelle He
María del Carmen Hernández
Suh Heui
Ryan Hillstead
JoJo Hong
Cindy Huang
Mie Inoue
Chiami Inoue
SoYun Jeong
Verónica Jiménez
Qi Jing
Sunshui Jing
Maiko Kainuma
YoungJin Kang
Chisato Kariya
Yoko Kato
Eriko Kawada
Sanae Kawamoto
Sarah Ker
Sheely Ker
Hyomin Kim
Lee Knight
Akiyo Kumazawa
JinJu Lee
Eunchae Lee
Jin-Yi Lee
Sharlene Liao
Yu Ya Link
Marcela Marluchi
Hilda Martínez Rosal
Alejandro Mateos Chávez
Cristina Medina Gómez
Bertha Elsi Méndez
Luz del Carmen Mercado
Ana Morales
Ana Estela Morales
Zita Morales Cruz
Shinano Murata
Junko Nishikawa
Sawako Ogawa
Ikuko Okada
Hiroko Okuno
Tomomi Owaki
Sayil Palacio Trejo
Rosa Lilia Paniagua
MiSook Park
SeonJeong Park
JoonYong Park
María Eugenia Pastrana
Silvia Santana Paulino
Dulce María Pineda
Rosalinda Ponce de León
Liliana Porras
María Elena Portugal
Yazmín Reyes
Diana Rivas Aguilar
Rosa Rivera Espinoza
Nayelli Guadalupe Rivera Martínez
Araceli Rivero Martínez
David Robin
Angélica Rodríguez
Leticia Santacruz Rodríguez
Silvia Santana Paulino
Kate Sato
Cassie Savoie
Mark Savoie
Yuki Scott
Yoshiko Shimoto
Jeehye Shin
MiYoung Song
Lisa Styles
Laura Sutton
Mayumi Tabuchi
Takako Takagi
Miriam Talonia
Yoshiko Tanaka
María Isabel Tenorio
Chioko Terui
José Francisco Trenado
Yasuko Tsujimoto
Elmer Usaguen
Hiroko Usami
Michael Valentine
José Javier Vargas
Nubia Margot Vargas
Guadalupe Vázquez
Norma Velázquez Gutiérrez
Ruth Marina Venegas
María Martha Villegas Rodríguez
Heidi Wang
Tomiko Watanabe
Jamie Wells
Susan Wu
Junko Yamaguchi
Dai Yang
Judy Yao
Yo Yo
Sally Yu
Mary Zhou
Rose Zhuang

Stickers

Quest

Unit 1 My toys

page 18

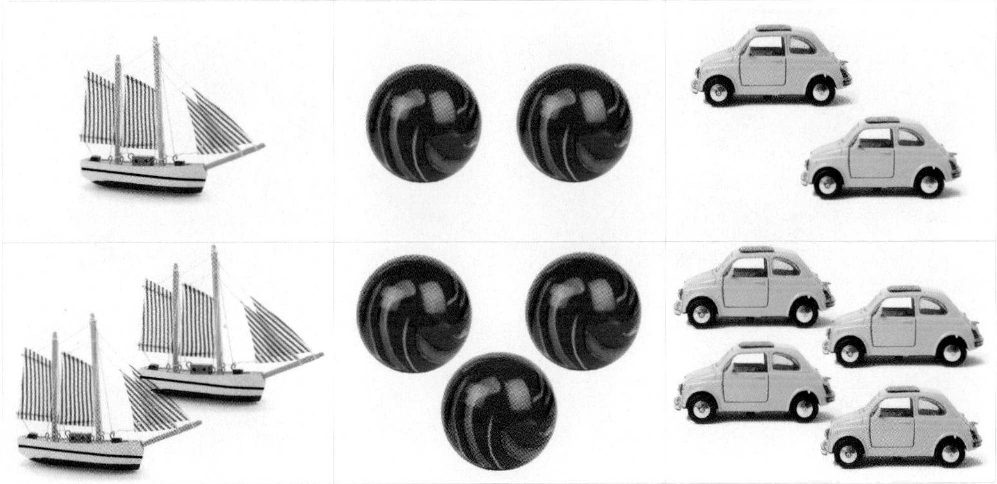

Unit 2 My family

page 24

Unit 3 **Move your body**

page 39

Unit 4 **My face**

page 46

Unit 5 **Animals**

page 58

page 61

Unit 6 Food

page 69

Unit 7 Clothes

page 81

page 83

I'm sorry. Goodbye! Good morning.

Good night. Please. Thank you.

Unit 8 Weather

page 90